John Ellis Edwards

The Confederate soldier

Being a memorial sketch of George N. and Bushrod W. Harris

John Ellis Edwards

The Confederate soldier
Being a memorial sketch of George N. and Bushrod W. Harris

ISBN/EAN: 9783337118884

Printed in Europe, USA, Canada, Australia, Japan

Cover: Foto ©ninafisch / pixelio.de

More available books at **www.hansebooks.com**

THE

CONFEDERATE SOLDIER;

BEING

A MEMORIAL SKETCH

OF

GEORGE N. AND BUSHROD W. HARRIS
PRIVATES IN THE CONFEDERATE ARMY.

BY

REV. JOHN E. EDWARDS, A. M., D. D.

NEW YORK:
BLELOCK & CO., 453 BROOME STREET.
1868.

To the Memory of

THE PRIVATE SOLDIERS IN THE LATE CONFEDERATE ARMY
WHO SLEEP IN THEIR HUMBLE GRAVES,
KNOWN AND UNKNOWN;

AND

TO THE LIVING SOLDIERS WHO SERVED AS PRIVATES
IN THE RANKS, AND WHO NOW WEAR THEIR SCARS
AS BADGES OF HONOR IN THE PRIVATE AND
USEFUL WALKS OF LIFE,

THIS LITTLE VOLUME

IS RESPECTFULLY DEDICATED BY A

BEREAVED FATHER.

PREFACE.

The following sketch has been prepared from a very limited amount of material. A few pages of manuscript, containing an account of the boyhood and early youth of the "*Twin Brothers*," together with some brief notes of their short career as private soldiers in the Confederate Army, during the first year of the war, to which was added the certificates and testimonials of officers and personal friends, as to their gallantry and heroism in the camp and in the field, formed the entire stock out of which the author has attempted to construct this little volume. He has therefore taken the liberty of weaving into the web of the narrative various facts and events of coincident history, and has even gone so far as to extend the line of remark to incidents which transpired at a later period of time than that embraced in the brief history of the immediate subjects of this memorial offering. The object of the author has been to bring out, with some degree of prominence, the life of the soldier who occupied the position of *a private in the ranks*, during the Confederate struggle for Southern independence. A more gallant, valorous, self-sacrificing, and patriotic soldiery never met an invading foe, than graced the rank and file of the Confederate army. Their deeds deserve to be chronicled on brass and marble, and their names preserved on the scroll of historic fame, while true patriotism has an altar, or civil liberty a temple, in the onward roll of the ages.

The preparation of this memorial sketch, while it has been undertaken at the urgent request of a bereaved father, has, nevertheless, been performed as "a labor of love." The author has taken a pride and a pleasure in paying this merited tribute to the memory and virtues of the two young men who form the special subjects of this sketch, as it has furnished an occasion and opportunity for saying some things that have not been said of the private soldiers composing the rank and file of the late Confederate army. Hence, the work has been expanded from a mere biographical sketch, of a few pages, in which the material points in the brief history of these youthful soldiers might have been recorded, into a small volume. These young men have been regarded as mere specimens of their class. Viewed in this light, no apology is necessary for the latitude which has been taken in the range of remark and observation indulged by the writer. Others than the immediate circle of relatives and friends of the "Twin-Brothers" may find something to engage their attention in this unpretending volume.

THE AUTHOR.

LYNCHBURG, Virginia, July, 1868.

CHAPTER I.

THE heroic deeds of the great military leaders in the late Confederate struggle for independence *have been* and *will be* duly chronicled. The historian will recount *their* feats of valor upon the glowing page for the generations to come. Their deeds of chivalry and daring will live, invested with the charm of romance, when the busy fingers of time shall have effaced their names from the monumental marble reared by the hand of affection to perpetuate and transmit their memories from age to age, adown the lapse of oncoming centuries. The names of Generals, and Colonels, and Majors, with here and there the name of an inferior officer who distinguished himself by some noteworthy and valorous deed, will be preserved; but the *names* and heroic deeds of the humble private in the ranks will remain unrecorded, and unsung, except in a few isolated cases where the hand of affection is put forth to rescue the name and memory from the vortex of oblivion. The polished shaft, with its eulogistic inscription, will mark the spot and commemorate the fame of the chieftain, while the ploughshare shall be driven over the sleeping dust of the brave and gallant private, who bared his breast in the battle strife, and fell, "with his back to the field, and his feet to the foe."

The Confederate army, taken as a whole, had a larger proportion of polished, refined, and educated young *gentlemen*, in its rank and file, than ever graced the columns of any other army that ever took the field, in ordinary warfare, between belligerent powers. The flower and chivalry of the Southern States stood shoulder to shoulder in the ranks. Young men who had been contestants for literary distinction in the colleges and universities of our own land, and who had shared the honors of the universities of Europe, were found side by side in the long and weary march, foot to foot in the fight, and sharers of the same scanty rations in the camp. These young men had been accustomed, from childhood, to all the elegancies, and luxuries, and refinements of the highest social life in the South. They had been educated for the various learned professions, or reared up in the counting room, or had given themselves up to lives of indolent ease and pleasure. When the tocsin of war was sounded, by a common impulse, they threw aside their books, closed their offices, forsook the halls of learning, turned away from the haunts of pleasure—

doffed the citzen's dress, donned the Confederate gray, and hastened with their comrades in arms to hurl back the proud invader from our southern soil. In a few brief months these patriotic and gallant young men were so transformed by the hardships and privations of the soldier's life, that the mother's quick eye could scarcely detect a lineament of the smooth and youthful face of the fair-haired, or dark-eyed boy that left her in the buoyancy and ardor of early life for the camp and the field.

Who shall write the history of these young men? What gifted pen shall portray, in adequate forms of expression, the lives of the confederate soldiery? Alas for them, the *names* of thousands of them, like their *graves*, are unknown! They passed through every conceivable phase of the soldier's life during a long and bloody war. Dreary winters were spent in the camp; parching summers in the field. Days, together, were passed without any kind of food, except a handful of meal, or a little parched corn. Acorns and wild haws, and even the inner bark of the trees were sometimes resorted to for the purpose of appeasing gnawing hunger. They were often, indeed more frequently than otherwise, poorly clad. Their feet were bare, and their heads without a covering. Bronzed, burnt, and blistered by the scorching sun, they trudged under the burden of rifle, knapsack, and cartridge box during the day, and slept on the bare ground during the night. Often, broken down by disease, or mangled in battle, they were borne on litters to the hospital to linger and die. How many thousands of these noble young men breathed their last expiring gasp, within gloomy walls, on the unfurnished bunk, without a look of love, or a tone of sympathy to soothe the parting hour! How many were laid in rough pine boxes, or wrapped in tattered blankets, and tumbled, without a tear, into the ground, and the place of interment left without a stone to mark the spot where the hero sleeps! Whole brigades slumber in Hollywood and Oakwood Cemeteries, near Richmond. Thousands upon thousands in the burying grounds of Lynchburg, and Petersburg, and Gordonsville, and Charlottesville, and Danville, Virginia; to say nothing of the multiplied thousands that lie scattered, almost as thick as autumn leaves, on the lines of march, marked by the footprints of the army, or hastily and carelessly interred on gory battle-fields when the conflict was ended, and the victory won. Who can number the graves that once heaved the soil near Chattanooga, at Shiloh, on the hills around Gettysburg, along the banks of the Potomac and Rappahannock; at Charleston, South Carolina; near Newbern, and Washington, and Plymouth, and Kinston, and Wilmington, and Beaufort, North Carolina?

"Memorial Associations" have been formed by the patriotic women of the South for the purpose of rescuing these graves, as far as may be, from the levelling hand of time. Thousands upon thousands, by the interposition of these friendly hands, have been marked by head-boards, bearing the name, and company, and regiment of the sleeper beneath. The mound has again been raised above the ashes of the manly form of the soldier that fought and fell far from his kindred and home; and, with the annual return of the season of flowers, wreaths of roses, and spring-blossoms, entwined with evergreens, and often bedewed with tears, are laid, by fair hands, upon these graves, nursed and cared for by woman's love.

The private soldier, in the Confederate service, was often a man of mark—a representative man; and, while the rank and file, generally, were made up of superior material, there were very many, who never rose above the position of a non-commissioned officer, who are as much entitled, on account of their bravery and daring as soldiers, to a conspicuous place in history, as others who commanded a brigade, or division, or even stood at the head of an army corps.

The *officer* in command gets the praise for the victories won by his veteran soldiery. His name is embalmed in song—his deeds are trumpeted to the world—his likeness occupies a prominent place in the photograph album—his prowess, bravery and skill are lauded to the echo, and chronicled for the world; but, not a name of a single soldier who breasted the leaden hail, who mounted the breastworks, who wrenched down the enemies' flag, who trampled down the foe, and drove him from the field, finds a place on the scroll of fame, or receives a note of applause from the hero-worshippers of the age. We are not bitter against the spirit that awards the just meed of praise to the military leader; on the contrary, we approve and appreciate it. The chieftain should be held in grateful remembrance by those for whom he planned, and fought, and fell. The officers who survive the conflict, and yet, who bore themselves well in the army; who shared the fortunes of the soldiery; who bravely met the foe, and did not shrink from duty or danger; who stood firmly by the cause at stake, and sacrificed every thing for its maintenance and success: such men are worthy of all praise.

It would be a shame and a reproach if posterity were to permit such names to perish. The memory of such men as Lee, and Jackson, and Sidney Johnston, and others that might be added to the list should be kept fresh and fragrant in the hearts of the Southern people, and bequeathed as a precious and valuable legacy to their children's children. But while we perpetuate the names and achievements of the noble men who commanded our armies, we should not allow the names of the no less noble and self-sacrificing soldiers, who occupied a place in the ranks, to sink into forgetfulness. It is a duty we owe to those who bore the brunt of the battle; who lived on the hard fare, and received the poor pay; who sacrificed fortune, home, health, and life itself in the defence of a cause that we deemed just—it is a duty we owe to their memories—to their patriotism and heroism, to snatch their names from the wave that bears them to oblivion, and fix them

"As lights and landmarks on the cliffs of fame."

It is in obedience to this behest of duty and affection that we have undertaken to record, in brief outline, a memorial sketch of two young men who acted their part in the late Confederate war. The story is brief, and not distinguished by any thing out of the ordinary way, except, perhaps, in a single particular hereafter to be chronicled. Ten thousand similar records might be written as to the main facts of their history. Many, very many, fought in more battles than did these young men. Others, and not a few, performed equally notable and conspicuous service, except in the instance referred to above; and yet, *parental love* wishes, in this more permanent form, to continue their names, and to hold up their example, at least, before the eyes of a circle of friends and relatives, as a tribute of affection to their memory and virtues.

The reader, then, will bear in mind that this little book is *in memoriam ;* that it is a fadeless wreath of simple flowers—the flowers of affection, laid upon the graves of two dear sons, by the trembling hands of an aged father and mother, as a testimonial of that love which can never die—a father's and a mother's love.

CHAPTER II.

GEORGE NELSON and BUSHROD WASHINGTON HARRIS, twin brothers, and sons of George W. and Martha M. Harris, were born in Albemarle County, Virginia, January 11th, 1842.

George W. Harris, the father of the subjects of this biographical and historical sketch, was the son of Capt. Benjamin Harris of Revolutionary memory. Capt. Harris was an officer in the Revolutionary war; he was at Yorktown at the surrender of Cornwallis, and was frequently in the society of General Washington, while engaged in military service. For Washington he formed a strong personal attachment. His admiration of the great chieftain's exalted character was unbounded. This may account for the fact that his son, the father of George and Bushrod Harris, bears the name of WASHINGTON; and he, in his turn, imbibing in early life the sentiments of his Revolutionary father in relation to the noble "father of his country," gave to each of the twin brothers a part of Washington's name. He was a great admirer also of the life and character of Lord Admiral Nelson. In early life his mind was singularly impressed with the naval exploits of this distinguished officer, and on this account he gave the name of Nelson to one of the twin sons.

The father says he never could satisfactorily account for the strange transposition of names—George *Nelson*, and Bushrod *Wash-*

ington, instead of Bushrod Nelson and George Washington. The leading traits of character subsequently developed in young *Nelson* showed, as he thinks, that if the father was not guided by a power above him in giving this name to the child, as Jacob of old was directed in the bestowment of his blessing upon the sons of Joseph, there was, at least, an accidental appropriateness in the name thus given.

These twin brothers were favored with devoted, Christian parents, who, from early infancy, labored, by precept and example, to mould their characters for future usefulness. Their infant lips were taught to lisp the Lord's Prayer. Their young and inexperienced feet were restrained from turning into the paths of sin, and carefully conducted into the ways of uprightness, integrity, and truth. The lessons impressed upon their infantile and youthful minds and hearts were not effaced by the wear and tear of after years; but remained, as if written on adament with a pen of diamond, and continued, through life, to exert a salutary and controlling influence upon their conduct, characters, and conversation. A mother's lessons, taught to her child in early life, are written with sympathetic ink upon the leaflets of the heart and memory; and although for a season she may not be able to trace the effects upon the life, yet, by and by, when exposed to the heat and buffetings of more advanced years, the characters will be drawn out, and the lessons will be found to be as imperishable as the immortal mind on which they are written.

The two brothers were strikingly alike in person, and also in the mental and moral traits early displayed in their lives. They spent their time in each other's society, and seemed to be a part and parcel of each other. The resemblance of their features was so strong—so exactly alike, that even their nurses, in childhood, and their parents and other members of the household, at a later day, frequently mistook the one for the other. As they grew older, mistakes of this sort became a source of amusement to them, and they frequently practised the little deception of misleading their friends and acquaintances on this subject for the sake of the merriment which it afforded them.

It would be a useless consumption of the reader's time to enter into a detailed account of the thousand and one little incidents of childhood and youth, as they stand connected with the lives of the subjects of this memorial sketch. They acquired a knowledge of letters at an early period of life; passed through the ordinary routine of an elementary training, escaping, in a remarkable degree, the birch and willow which falls to the lot of most boys without stint. They mingled in the sports of the play ground; had an occasional skirmish at fisticuffs with their school-fellows, in which they generally got the best of it. This was true especially of *Bush*, as he was called, who was of a more impulsive and fiery temper than George. Both of them had inherited high-spirited natures from the father's side of the family. In boyhood they claimed and defended their rights. *Bush*, with his quick and less governable temper, would brook no insult, and was thus more frequently brought into collision with his teachers and school-mates than his brother. He never failed to vindicate his honor, however slightly impeached; and, although it might subject him to reprimand by the teacher, or expulsion from the school by the trustees, he fearlessly met the consequences. A jeer or a flout, directed against himself, or any member of his family, was sure to meet with a spirited rebuff from *Bush*. In all his difficulties and rencounters, however, with his preceptors or school-fellows, he was always found to have such just ground for his positions as to vindicate himself in the estimation of his father. With this he was content. His father's approval was his panoply and pride. He was honorable and truthful and high-minded himself, and he could not and would not tolerate any thing in others that, in his estimation, involved a violation of the principles of honor and manliness that ought to govern even boys in their association and intercourse one with another. George was not less elevated and correct in his principles of action; but, being less ardent and impulsive in his nature, he was more conciliatory, and less hasty in his temper, words, and actions than his brother *Bush*.

Their vacations, and other intervals from study and school exercises, were spent in fishing, hunting, and the sports of the field. In their rambles, and other excursions through wood and field, they caught inspiration from the scenery which greeted their eyes on every hand. Mountains, in endless chains, swept around them. Landscapes of unrivalled beauty, made up of cultivated fields, dotted with clumps of stately trees, skirted with forest-crowned hills, and inlaid with flowing streams, lay near at hand; while, in the background, the many-colored mountains, with their ever-varying hues of blue and purple, formed the framework of a picture that would have fascinated the eye and thrilled the heart of a Claude Lorraine, a Church, or a Turner.

The healthful and invigorating exercises in which they indulged in the intervals of study, surrounded as they were by the beautiful and enchanting scenery of one of the most picturesque sections of Virginia, had the effect to develop the physical, in harmony with the intellectual elements of their natures; while the home influences, which were of a high, moral tone, countervailed any vicious tendencies that might have gained a temporary ascendency during their absence from the paternal roof, by their contact and association with the crowd of boys in a mixed and miscellaneous country or village school. The mother's eye was quick to detect any indication of the slightest departure from the paths of virtue and Christian purity in which she had taught their young and inexperienced feet to tread. Her pious example and oft-repeated admonitions checked the wayward tendencies of their early youth, and led them to adopt the moralities of the Decalogue, and the precepts of the Great Teacher as the rule of their conduct. Under the teachings of that *mother*, enforced by the example of the father, profanity was checked upon the lips of these twin-brothers; sabbath-breaking was corrected by an appeal to the word of God; hypocrisy, deceit, and dishonesty were taught to be as sinful in the sight of God as they are disreputable in the estimation of all right-minded men; integrity, truthfulness, and honor were enforced as *Christian* virtues, rather than as mere conventionalities; and their minds and hearts were duly impressed with the conviction that, true religion, in the *Bible* sense, is the best and only safeguard of virtue, while it is, in fact "the highest style of man." A *mother*, who had read her Bible through, year by year, for the space of well-nigh forty years; who was, herself, the model of every Christian virtue; whose daily walk was consistent with her religious profession, and whose heart was deeply imbued with all the charities and gentleness of the gospel, while it was full of the affection and devotion of the best of mothers, was a fitting teacher of such lessons to her sons. Under this home-tuition, fixed principles of conduct were early established in the minds of these youths. Their consciences became responsive to truth, and moral duty; and, in sending them from home, their parents had a high sense of assurance that the principles of rectitude imbedded in the minds of their sons would prove an overmatch for the allurements of vice and the solicitations of sinful associates, when thrown out into the world, and from under the eye, and away from the watch-care of home. Nor were they disappointed in this expectation. In 1860 we find these brothers at school with the Rev. Joseph A. Daniel, at Sharon, in Albemarle county, where they won the affection and esteem of the teacher, and of the scholars, and made rapid advances in their respective studies.

They were now verging on early manhood. Their habits were formed. They had passed the perils of youth in safety, and with high credit to themselves, to their parents and instructors. In manners and general deportment they were unexceptionable. On the approach to manhood they still bore a most remarkable resemblance to each other in person, and, with the exception before alluded to, in respect to the impulsiveness of temper and precipitancy in action, they were strikingly alike in mind and morals. They seemed, really, to be the counterpart of each other. Most of their time was passed in each other's society. Whether in the schoolroom, in the social circle, or engaged in outdoor amusements and the sports of the field or play-ground, they seemed inseparable. Perhaps the instances have been exceedingly rare in which two brothers ever loved each other more tenderly. They ate, and slept, and walked together; and even a temporary separation was painful to them. It is wonderful how much and how tenderly two members of the same household may love each other! The love and union of these two brothers was a subject of general remark, and was, in itself, a beautiful moral spectacle. Their last teacher, the Rev. Mr. Daniel, was looking to an opening in Shenandoah county, Virginia, for the establishment of a school; and, so well pleased was he with the habits and scholarship of George that he offered him, on certain contingencies, the position of assistant in his school. These contingencies, however, it would seem, did not occur; and, on the breaking up of the school at Sharon, the brothers, George, and Bushrod, each sought a situation as teacher, and were soon established at the head of their respective schools, in Rockingham county, Virginia. They were young and inexperienced in teaching, and yet so assiduously did they apply themselves to their work of instruction, and so considerate were they of the claims of their pupils, and so attentive to all their wants, that they soon gained the confidence and respect of their patrons, and won the affection and esteem of their scholars. But their career as teachers was brief. In the midst of this noble and praiseworthy employment they were suddenly aroused by the war-cry that rang through the land. Instantly their patriotic blood was fired; and, casting aside the ferule and birch, they hastened homeward for the purpose of offering themselves as volunteers in defence of what they regarded the *rights* of their State. The proud and insolent invader was threatening to march through Virginia, on his way to put down, with force of arms, the revolutionary movements of the more Southern states ; and these young men, with the pride and flower of the Old Dominion, generally, felt that they must make common cause with the insulted South.

From early childhood they had been accustomed to hear the stories connected with the Revolutionary struggle, in which their grandfather was an actor. They had heard their father recount the incidents of camp life; the fierce conflicts on bloody battle-fields ; the hardships attendant on long and weary marches ; the adventures connected with the siege of Yorktown, together with the triumph of that grand event which closed the protracted war—the surrender of Lord Cornwallis, as he had received these incidents from his father's lips. The early aspirations for military life, engendered by these recitals, and subsequently fostered by the example and teachings of their own father, who always displayed a fondness for military tactics and fame, had fully prepared these young men to leap, with a bound, to the first call of their country to shoulder the musket, and enter the ranks for its defence. The *names* given them, also, by that patriotic father, no doubt, had its effect in awakening in their minds a desire to imitate the example of the great prototypes set before them—Washington and Nelson. They were naturally led to read every thing that related to the lives and achievements of two of the greatest and noblest military men that have won for themselves a world-wide renown—the one in the Army, and the other in the Navy. It is not wonderful then that these youths—for they were but eighteen years of age, should be found among the first that offered themselves for the defence of the South.

CHAPTER III.

OUR memorial sketch has conducted us to the spring of 1861. The war-cloud that had, at first, shown itself as a mere speck upon the horizon, and which for a while awakened no very serious apprehension in the popular mind, now suddenly expanded its dark, portentous folds over the whole heavens. Strange as it may, and will, appear to the reader of history in the future, it is nevertheless true that the secession of South Carolina, followed as it was, in a short time, by the secession of other States, did not really arouse the great masses of the people to the apprehension of the imminency of a protracted and terrible war. Nor was it, indeed, until Virginia was called on by executive proclamation from Washington to raise its quota of men to suppress the revolutionary movements in the seceded States, that the people began to realize that war was really inaugurated, and that blood was to be shed. And even then, except with the more thinking and sagacious, it was thought that, after a slight skirmish at arms, the war-cloud would be borne away by the breath of peace, bearing upon its retiring skirts the beautiful bow which should be the pledge, in all time, of friendly and brotherly relations between the North and South. But very soon these hopes were dissipated. Thicker and darker the clouds became, as months and years glided away; nor did the storm abate its force till the whole land was desolated. The floods still cover the highest mountains, and no Ararat yet peers above the turbid waters, offering a spot of repose for the battered and weatherworn ship of state.

We drop back to the month of April, 1861. Among the very first companies that were organized for the purpose of meeting the advancing foe, just now ready to put his foot on Virginia soil, was the "Howardsville Grays," known, at a later day, as Company D, of the 19th Regiment of Virginia volunteers. This company was organized and drilled by Captain J. J. Hopkins, of Albemarle County.

The two brothers, George and Bushrod Harris, as we have seen, had given up their schools and returned to their home in Albemarle. They signified their purpose to volunteer at once in defence of the State. Parental feelings were interposed. Mother and sisters earnestly, and with tears and entreaties, besought them, at least for the nonce, to abandon their purpose. But tears and entreaties were all in vain. Their father, seeing that it was useless to oppose their wishes, and being himself a patriotic and military man, proposed to accompany them to Howardsville, the headquarters of Captain Hopkins' company. On presenting themselves for enlistment, the captain informed them that his ranks were full, and that he had neither arms nor uniforms for any additional recruits. Furthermore, he said he was too unwell to drill the company, and decidedly advised them to return home, and to desist, for the present at least, from joining any military organization. Having done what they felt to be a duty, and failing, as it would seem, to accomplish their object, their father persuaded them now to be satisfied for the present, and to return home with him, and patiently await for some other opportunity to volunteer. But before leaving for home, the father, with his sons, went to the grounds where the company was drilling, and, such was the effect upon those gallant youths, as they saw many of their youthful companions, and others of their countrymen in the ranks, marching and countermarching, that they involuntarily burst into tears at their own disappointment. Seeing this, the officers and men determined that a place should be made for them in the company. The father's consent was freely and fully given. The vote of the company was taken on their reception. When it was announced that the *boys* were received, there was an outburst of enthusiasm. Hats flew into the air, huzzas and shouts rang out until the hills gave back the echo, and the noble youths were duly enrolled as members of the company.

The following is a copy of the certificate given by Captain Hopkins, the original of which will be sacredly preserved as a sort of heir-loom, to be handed down from sire to son in the Harris family:

"I certify that on the 17th April, 1861, I enlisted, among others, George N. Harris, and his brother, Bushrod W. Harris, in my company which was preparing to repel the invader of our soil. I was in command of the said company about one month, during which time I was particularly struck with the soldier-like conduct of these young men, who gave great promise of usefulness to our cause, and was not at all surprised when I heard of their chivalrous bearing in the hour of battle. They deserve to live in the hearts of their countrymen.

(Signed) "J. J. HOPKINS."

It is difficult for us, after the intervention of a long and tragic war, marked by violence and murderous deeds, with its record of hard-fought battles, imprisonments, and sufferings in camp and hospitals; its horrid oppressions, hardships, conscriptions, and its endless list of unparalleled atrocities—it is difficult to recall and appreciate the *feelings* with which we viewed the initiation of the war, and the first stages of the fearful and desperate struggle. Our people at last became accustomed to that which, at first, from its novelty, and other elements of interest, affected them deeply and strangely. We were moved to tears by incidents and events that occurred at the commencement of the war, which, at a later day, would scarcely have awakened a solitary emotion. Indeed, there were events, and not a few, that then excited the deepest interest in the public mind, that are now recalled with a smile and a jeer. Panics were occasioned by things that now appear to have been superlatively ridiculous. But, going back to the opening of the war, we can now recall many scenes that were touching and heart-rending. Time can never obliterate them from the memory, or extract from them the elements that have fastened them to the heart forever. Tears still dim the eye, as we look back upon them through the mists and gloom of the sad and sorrowful years that have rolled between those events and the present hour. We then saw the beardless boy, with his fair skin and delicate hand, who had never spent a night in the open field, gird on his knapsack, shoulder his heavy rifle, and start for the camp. A mother's tearful eye followed his departing footsteps—alas! too often, footsteps departing to return no more. We have seen the young husband tear himself from the clinging embrace of his beautiful bride, and hasten away to bear his part in the defence of his country.

Well do we now remember the day on which the "Home Guards," the old "Rifle Grays," "Latham's Battery," and other companies, forming afterward a part of the 11th Regiment, Virginia volunteers, left the city of Lynchburg for Richmond, to swell the

Confederate army then organizing for active campaigning in the field. Long before the hour for the departure of the cars, which were to bear these noble companies away from the Hill City, thousands of the citizens had assembled at the depot to witness the parting scene. Fathers and mothers, and wives and sisters, were there to exchange farewells with sons, and husbands, and brothers, many of whom were to be seen and looked upon for the last time. The companies came, and were soon packed in the crowded cars. The whistle gave the signal for starting. There was the shout of the soldiers, with the waving of handkerchiefs, and an attempt at a huzza on the part of the assembled multitude; but, as the cars moved away, there was heard the shriek and the wail of agonized and bleeding hearts. Wives and mothers swooned away as if dead. The crowd dispersed in cries and tears. Bitter wailings and lamentations were heard along the streets. Suppressed sobs and stifled groans were heard as if coming from broken hearts, while a pall of gloom seemed to settle over the city. Silence and sadness marked the passing hours of that day. Similar scenes transpired all over the Southern States. The romance that, for a brief space, invested the soldier's life in camp with a fascination and a charm, soon faded like the aurora-tints of the morning, to be followed by the dust, and heat, and toil of the advancing day.

To return to the subjects of this sketch: The father left the boys in camp, and hastened homeward to prepare an outfit for them in their new vocation as soldiers. In his lonely ride, his heart grew sick and sad as he thought of the probable fortunes of his sons in the on-coming conflict. He was advancing in years. His sons were his pride, and the light of his home. He must meet a sorrowing and disconsolate mother on his return to his household circle. It was the painful struggle of parental love and *feeling* with a high-toned patriotism that could withhold no sacrifice for the honor and defence of the State. When the family assembled that evening to engage in the religious worship with which they were accustomed to close the day, the utterances of the father were choked and broken as he attempted to offer prayer for the absent sons. The mother and sisters and younger brothers gave themselves up to sobs and tears. How many fathers and mothers, at the commencement of the war, bedewed their pillows with their tears the first night that their soldier boy spent in camp! How earnest were the prayers that went up from family altars for the members of the household who for the first time were absent from their accustomed places at the time of the morning and evening devotions! In no home circle was there a severer conflict, in parting with sons, during this trying period, that in the home of Colonel Harris, on the occasion of the enlistment of his boys as we have recited in the foregoing part of this chapter.

The "Howardsville Grays" continued to rendezvous for several weeks at the little town of Howardsville on James river. Captain Hopkins was compelled, on account of his health, to surrender the command of the company, but he never lost his interest in its welfare. He watched its history and fortunes with a jealous eye. He was succeeded in command by Captain Josiah Faulkner, who filled the office with distinguished gallantry, and skill; and won for himself the confidence and respect of his company.

While in camp at Howardsville the company, in the intervals of the drill and other military exercises, gave themselves up to pastimes, and sports of various kinds. A band was employed to regale them with music. Night after night was passed in the singing of glee-songs, and in other mirthful amusements. The religious education, and the conscientious scruples of the new recruits,

George, and Bushrod Harris, would not allow them to participate in these frivolous and worldly diversions, as they regarded them. They had been reared in a school of severe morals, under the tuition of a pious mother, and they were too true to the principles of their education, and too respectful to the known wishes and religious convictions of that mother, to yield to the solicitations of their comrades, in running into any excess in camp, in which they would not indulge under their mother's eye. With the solemn conviction that

> "It is not all of life to live,
> Nor all of death to die,"

and with the further conviction that the profession of arms does not absolve one from the obligations of private morality, they did not allow themselves, as Christian young men, to indulge in any thing that they would not have regarded as perfectly innocent and proper in the private walks of life. They started out with a purpose, which they unflinchingly maintained under all the allurements and fascinations of vice, to preserve their Christian integrity unimpeached and irreproachable to the end. The jeer of a messmate, on account of their religious scruples, was too weak a weapon to dislodge them from the rock of virtue on which they stood; and the sneer of an official, even, was too impotent to shake them from their abiding adherence to high moral resolve. They wore their virtue, not as a mask, but as a shield. Their line of conduct was not shaped and governed by policy or caprice, but by principle and piety. They did not regard the life of a soldier as being incompatible with the maintenance of the highest and purest morality; and the brief career of these young men fully vindicated the views which they boldly and fearlessly avowed.

The "Howardsville Grays," after the lapse of·a few weeks, moved from Howardsville to Charlottesville, preparatory to a further advance in the direction of Alexandria. Here they spent a short time in perfecting their organization for the active campaign which was now fully on foot for the approaching summer. The Confederate army which had been massing at Richmond was getting ready for the field. Southern troops which had congregated at Lynchburg were waiting orders to go forward to meet the enemy. The whole country was now in a state of the highest excitement and enthusiasm. The soldiers were in their new uniforms. Camps were kept in order, and, with the long rows and squares of snowy-white tents, and the throngs of officers and men mingling together, without any marked distinction of rank except the badges and insignia of office, presented the spectacle of a holiday picnic party, or the brilliancy and gayety of a bazaar or agricultural fair. Evening parades were graced by the elegance and beauty of city and country. Soldiers of every grade were invited everywhere to share the hospitalities of private families. Bouquets of the richest flowers were thrown indiscriminately by the hands of mothers and maidens upon the passing groups of soldiers. Weeks were passed at this stage of the great Confederate movement as a succession of gala-days. The hours of the night were winged with festive song, and serenade. Our soldiers knew but little or nothing of restraint or military discipline. Every young man was expecting to distinguish himself as a hero, and soon to return from the wars, with his clustering honors fresh upon his brow, to claim the plighted hand of his lady-love. Every body was hopeful, and sanguine of success. In a few months our Southern independence was to be fully achieved, and the sunny South was to flourish like a garden, and become the glory of all lands. "King Cotton" was to rule the world. The cause was just, and it was believed that God would vindicate the right.

The transition from the quiet and peaceful pursuits of life to a state of war, with all its exciting scenes, was sudden and unexpected. The change was violent. Business was arrested, and diverted into new channels. Farmers left their ploughs in the field; young men broke off from their studies, and from their professional callings, and hastened to unite with the volunteer companies, everywhere preparing for active service in the field. One wild scene of enthusiastic excitement spread over the whole country. Expectations were large. Extravagant forms of expression were employed. Every thing was magnified into huge and gigantic proportions. Our people really did not know what war meant. Years—long, dark bloody years—of carnage, death, and desolation taught us the meaning of that word, WAR. We learned its import and significance in hard-fought battles; in hospitals filled with the sick, the mangled, the mutilated and the dying; in long and weary marches; in bivouac and camp, through cold and dreary winters; in blockaded ports; in privation and want; in orphanage and widowhood; in desolated lands and smouldering ruins; in prostrated fortunes and heart-broken families; in the loss of those we most loved—the brave, the chivalrous, the heroic sons of the South, whose memory we cherish, and whose graves we hold sacred, and intend to bequeath as a precious legacy to the generations to come after us, with the injunction that the mothers and the maidens shall lay upon them the tribute of spring's brightest flowers while virtue has an altar, and patriotism a pulse that throbs in sympathy with the cause for which they sacrificed their noble lives. The lesson has been taught us. We know and feel what war is NOW.

The twin brothers had just returned to Charlottesville from a short and hurried visit of but a few hours, to their home, at Mountain Grove. They had left the paternal roof—and one of them for the last time—with a mother's blessing upon them, and with her counsels and admonitions ringing in their hearts and ears. Their father had accompanied them on their return to Charlottesville, the very day on which the company of which they were members was to move forward to Culpepper Court-house. Patriotic speeches had been delivered by various persons, on the eve of the departure of the cars; among others, Colonel Harris was called out for a speech. He spoke of the cause which our soldiery were to defend; of the hardships and trials that were before them; of the solemn obligation resting on every man to do his duty; and turning his eyes toward his boys, who stood in the ranks, with manly tears coursing down their cheeks, he said— "And you, my twin-born sons—bone of my bone, and flesh of my flesh,—I now 'commend to God, and the word of His grace, which is able to build you up, and give you an inheritance among them that are sanctified.' Do your *duty*, and the God of peace be with you." It was after this stirring and affecting scene, and while many were exchanging farewells with friends and relatives, that we find the brothers standing apart, and waiting for their father's farewell and blessing.

An eye-witness says, just before the cars moved off from the depot, Colonel Harris was seen standing by his sons, with a hand on the head of each, and with prayer and invocation offering them to God, and the service of their country. In a few moments the vanishing train had born the two companies away. With a sad heart, but still beating high with patriotic impulses and sentiments, the father wended his way to his home on the slope of the mountains. *Alta Vista* lay beneath his eye. Beyond and around were pictures of unrivalled loveliness and beauty. The fragrance of spring blossoms was in the air, and the minstrelsy of birds was ringing in the wildwood, while over all was heaven's high arch of matchless blue. Naught above, beneath or around, gave any indication to the quiet farmer, at his home among the hills, that bloody-handed war had mounted his murderous car, and was threatening to drive it ruthlessly over the fairest and happiest land under the sun. But from afar the troops were flocking to the point of conflict. The battle of Bethel was the first act in the bloody tragedy, and the world waited, with bated breath, for the renewed clangor of arms upon some more decisive and hard-fought field.

CHAPTER IV.

By the middle of May, 1861, a large number of Confederate troops had reached Manassas Junction. These were principally made up of the three-months South Carolina men. The 18th Regiment, Virginia volunteers, under command of Colonel Withers, was the first organized body of Virginia troops that reached Manassas, and the first to move forward to Centreville. The 19th Regiment did not receive its full complement of companies for some time after its organization. The "Howardsville Grays" and the "Scottsville Guards" went first to Culpepper Court-house, and thence to Manassas Junction, where they were thrown into the 19th Regiment, under the command, nominally, of Colonel Cocke, but really of Lieutenant-Colonel Strange, of Charlottesville. About the middle of June this regiment was moved forward to Centreville. The 18th Regiment, which had preceded the 19th to this point, for the purpose of relieving a South Carolina regiment, now moved forward as far as Fairfax Court-house, leaving the 19th on duty, with other regimental commands, at Centreville.

The " Howardsville Grays " lost its distinctive name on being merged into the regiment, and is henceforth to be known, in this narrative, as Company D of the 19th Regiment Virginia volunteers.

Here again we meet with the subjects of this memorial sketch. The highest expectations that have been awakened by their previous history, are not to be disappointed. The testimony of the officers in command is to the effect that the young brothers, George and Bushrod Harris were ever found ready to perform any service, or to take their turn on any post of duty to which they might be assigned. So far from shrinking from what was regarded as hard and perilous service, these young men courted it; not in the way of bluster and bravado, but in the spirit and temper of brave, quiet, unpretending youths, whose modesty was equal to their courage and valor. There were certain posts of picket duty that were deemed more perilous and exposed than others. These were sought in a quiet and modest way by George and Bushrod Harris. Captain Faulkner, under his own sign-manual, says:

"George N. and Bushrod W. Harris, members of my company, while stationed at Centreville, where picket duty was dangerous, always sought the *outer picket post. They shrank from no duty, and feared no danger.*"

As an instance of the courage and bravery of Bushrod W. Harris, we give the following well-authenticated fact in his brief history as a soldier. On one occasion an officer stated, while the company was in line, that he wanted three volunteers to fill responsible and dangerous stations. Every man held his position in the ranks, and profound silence reigned from right to left of the company. After a pause of a sufficient length of time for a response, and no one offering his services, the youthful Bushrod, with modesty advanced toward the officer, and timidly said he would be one of the number desired. When the company saw the youngest member on the roll, and nearly the last recruit stepping forward in response to this call, nearly the whole command instantly tendered their services.

On another occasion George was assigned to a picket post at a time when he was scarcely able to stand on his feet. Without a word he started to the point of duty. He was nearly blind from excruciating pain in his head, and staggered as he attempted to walk. A noble comrade, by the name of Samuel Thurmond, who was aware of his condition, said that no sick man should go on duty where he was, if he knew it; and instantly offered himself as a substitute for young Harris, which was accepted, and Harris was relieved from duty. This brave and generous soldier, SAMUEL THURMOND, fought through the first great battle of the war at Manassas. His health gave way. He was furloughed, and returned home, and soon thereafter died. The deeds of such noble men should be recorded in letters of gold on columns of adamant, to be preserved for the admiration of the ages to come.

In a very short time after going into camp at Centreville, the measles broke out among the soldiers. George and Bushrod Harris were both stricken down with the disease. George was attacked first, and was sent to the hospital at Culpepper Court-house. Here he remained but a short time, before he was again reported ready for service. He was not ready, in fact; but, because he was restless under the disease, and would be up, and walking about, perhaps in disregard of the advice of the surgeon, he was reported for duty. He returned to Centreville, and the day following his arrival in camp his brother Bushrod was attacked. The disease took violent hold of him, and being poorly provided for in the way of nursing and other attentions, the disease made rapid advances, and in the brief space of four days terminated fatally. From the commencement of the attack he said he would not recover. His mind was strongly impressed with the belief that he would die. He was confined in the stone church of the village then used as a hospital. Some kind ladies bestowed a share of attention upon him. For these attentions he was truly grateful, and requested his brother to return his thanks to the ladies for their care and kindness. He rapidly grew worse. His brother was too much enfeebled and prostrated by disease, from which he had not recovered, to bestow the attention upon Bushrod which his condition required. He, however, remained by him, and did all in his power to alleviate his sufferings, and relieve his wants. On the night of his death, he was restless but rational. He requested his brother who was lying on a bunk at his side, to read him at least one verse, if no more, from his Testament, which was under his pillow. He drew out the precious little book, which was soiled and worn from frequent perusal, and turning over its pages, by a happy selection his eyes fell on the 39th verse of the 10th chapter of the Epistle to the Hebrews, where it is written: "But, we are not of them who draw back unto perdition, but of them that believe to the saving of the soul." His heart and mind were firmly stayed on God. His hopes of a future state of recompense and reward were founded upon the Rock of Ages, and the apprehension of approaching dissolution could not shake him from his stronghold. Peacefully and hopefully he waited for the solemn change. He was taken ill on Wednesday, the 26th of June, and on the following Saturday night, June the 30th, he calmly sunk into the sleep of death. Without a struggle or a groan he yielded up his spirit into the hands of the God who gave it.

The death of Bushrod W. Harris was one of the first—if not *the* first—that occurred in the army at Centreville, certainly the first in this company. The soldiers had not yet become accustomed to the visitations of the destroyer. Their ranks had not as yet been decimated by the grape and canister of the enemy ; and while disease was growing rife in the army, and scores and hundreds were carried to the hospitals, death, up to this time, was a comparative stranger in the camp. On the occurrence of this death, the officers and men of the company were impressed and affected, and suitable arrangements were made for the return of the remains of young Harris to his family and friends in Albemarle. On the Monday following his death his body was deposited in a neat and tastefully decorated coffin, furnished, it would seem, by Lieutenant Carrington, and an escort of six soldiers detailed to attend the remains, with instructions to see them interred with military honors. George was also permitted to accompany his brother's corpse, and to witness the funeral solemnities at the time and place of interment.

The above-detailed events and occurrences had transpired at Centreville, without the knowledge of the parents and friends of the deceased at home. The first announcement of the sad intelligence of the death of Bushrod was by telegram, received on the day his remains were to arrive at the depot, in the neighborhood of the old homestead. The tidings, so sudden and unexpected, were crushing and heart-rending to the bereaved parents. They nevertheless tried to bow with resignation to the will of God, and with humble submission to repeat, "The Lord gave and the Lord hath taken away; blessed be the name of the Lord."

The remains were duly received at the depot, and conveyed across the country to Colonel Harris' residence. An appropriate funeral discourse was delivered on the occasion by the Rev. Adam C. Bledsoe, and then the lifeless lump of cold clay was borne to the family burying-ground for consignment to the house appointed for all the living. At the grave Captain Hopkins, who had charge of the "Howardsville Grays" at the time of young Harris' enlistment, made an appropriate address, pronouncing a beautiful and touching eulogy upon the young soldier, who had so early gone down to the grave without a stain or reproach upon his character. He spoke of his high sense of honor; of his soldier-like conduct; his dauntless courage; his rectitude of deportment, and his gentlemanly bearing. The open grave was alongside the grave of the older members of the family, who had long since passed away. In this the young soldier was deposited. The mound was raised above his sleeping dust. A military salute was fired by his comrades in arms, and then the sorrowing circle of friends and relations returned, leaving the youthful hero in his last resting-place beneath the silent sod. Sleep on, brave, noble young man. Thy sun has gone down at noon. Thy dreams of ambition have suddenly been dissipated by the solemn realities of eternity. The life and toils of the soldier have been exchanged for the life and rewards of a better land.

CHAPTER V.

GEORGE N. HARRIS, after attending the funeral services of his brother relapsed into a tenfold more painful and aggravated attack of disease than that which he had suffered from the measles in camp. The intense mental anguish through which he had passed in witnessing the sickness and death of a brother that he loved as tenderly as life itself, together with the fatigue and exposure attendant on the trip with his brother's remains, and the preparation for his burial, had utterly prostrated his physical strength, and laid him open to a most painful and protracted attack of disease, supervening on his attack of measles in the camp. During the continuance of this attack, which kept him confined for many weeks, all the symptoms were aggravated, and his sufferings intensified by his restless wish and desire to return to his company in the field. In his moments of partial delirium he tossed from side to side of his bed, and spoke wildly and incoherently of life in the camp. Six weeks of agonizing bodily suffering passed away before there was any abatement of the severity of the attack, or any prospect, the faintest, that he ever would recover. But the disease passed its crisis, and slowly and gradually he began to convalesce.

The summer had glided by, with its stirring events, and the autumn was far advanced before he could take the least out-door exercise, or bear the slightest exposure, or undergo the least fatigue. Such was the confidence of his Captain in his willingness to return to his command at the earliest practicable period, that he made no requisition upon him to report to any medical Board or other official, leaving it entirely to himself to report for duty when he felt himself sufficiently restored to take the field. It was not until late in April, 1862, that he found himself in a condition of health that justified his attempt to re-enter the service. He said that he had been kindly and indulgently treated by his officers, and that a sense of gratitude impelled him, without delay, as soon as he could travel, to return to his company.

What momentous events had transpired in the camp, and cabinet, and field since the surviving subject of this sketch followed the remains of his brother to the grave! One of the most splendidly equipped armies that ever took the field had met a most disastrous defeat on the hills and plains of Manassas. Shattered and broken, leaving their munitions of war, their army stores, their accoutrements and arms scattered on the line of retreat in promiscuous confusion, they had gone, cringing and crouching to Washington, while the Confederate army had gathered the spoils, and settled down in the quiet possession and enjoyment of a victory scarcely paralleled in the annals of modern warfare. The failure to improve the advantages acquired by this remarkable victory over a strong and powerful foe, protracted the conflict through years of carnage, to be ended at last in the overthrow of the Confederate cause, and in the utter ruin and desolation of one of the finest sections of the globe. But, "there's a divinity that shapes our ends," and shapes the fortunes and destinies of nations and governments, "rough hew them as we will." The proud pennon of the *Cumberland* had gone down in Hampton Roads, before the massive iron beak of the Merrimac. The old United States naval ships, that had traversed every sea, and displayed "the Stripes and Stars" in every maritime port of the world, had been made to seek protection under the rock-built walls and heavy guns of Fortress Monroe. The Confederate iron-clads and torpedoes had become the terror of the mighty ships and triple-turreted monitors of the Federal Navy. On land and water "the boys *in gray*" had proved an overmatch for "the boys in blue." In every contest the Confederates had been victorious. Norfolk and Portsmouth were still held by Confederate troops. Yorktown was considered impregnable. Wilmington and Charleston were steadily resisting all the efforts of the foe to capture and occupy them. Newbern and Plymouth were strong and defiant. Vicksburg was still holding out under the continuous rain of shot and shell, beating in a pitiless storm on that devoted city. All the Confederate strongholds were well manned and firmly held. Richmond was regarded as secure and safe from the hand of the spoiler. This was the state of affairs in the spring of 1862. But the Federal army had been thoroughly reorganized, and powerfully reinforced. McClellan's grand movement against Richmond was already fully inaugurated. His army was flocking in the direction of the Peninsula. The Confederate army was concentrating around Richmond. Grand but undeveloped preparations were on foot for the Spring and Summer campaign. This was the attitude of affairs at the time when we again fall back to take up the unpretending narrative which runs through this little book.

With the gradual recovery of his health, George made a few visits to his friends in the neighborhood. His deep and hidden grief, occasioned by the death of his brother, no doubt operated against his more rapid restoration to his former vigor and strength. He frequently alluded, in the presence of his family, to the sense of loneliness and isolation that oppressed him. He felt as though a part of himself had actually died, and had been buried; and yet he struggled hard to shake off the incubus and to rise above the paralyzing depression that weighed so heavily upon his spirits. A double responsibility now seemed to rest upon him. He felt that he must act a manly part for himself, and at the same time represent his brother in the battles of his country.

The winter had worn away. The balmy breath of spring was beginning to waken vegetation into life and motion. Soldiers who had enjoyed a brief furlough, with friends at home, were returning to the army. With the approach and advance of the vernal season the young invalid began to feel an increase of strength, and although opposed by the remonstrances and entreaties of friends, he determined to buckle on his armor and return to his command.

The 19th Regiment of Virginia Volunteers, to which his company belonged, by the changing fortunes of the army, was, at this time, at Yorktown; and George, with his youthful enthusiasm, was particularly anxious to re-enter the service while it was there, that he might tread the same *beats* that had been made sacred to his memory by the footprints of his grandfather, who had performed the duties of a Revolutionary soldier upon that historic soil. His preparations were accordingly made for his departure from home, again to take his part, as a private, in the Confederate service. He paid a parting visit to the grave of his brother, on which the tender grass and early spring flowers were beginning to peer above the sod. He bowed himself to the heaving mound; and while he reconsecrated himself to the service of God, he solemnly pledged himself afresh, and with renewed determination, to the service of his country. His patriotism caught a new impulse from the grave-stone of his venerated grandfather, and from the fresh-made grave of his brother, and from that hour, whatever might betide, for weal or for woe, he felt that, in his humble sphere, his fortunes were indissolubly linked with the fortunes and destiny of the Confederate cause. The foot of the enemy was on the soil of Virginia. A powerful and thoroughly equipped army, backed by the large resources of a great government, was threatening to crush the Southern States, and force them into allegiance to a dominant party that had trampled constitutional rights in the dust; and who, in utter disregard of the great principles which were defended and vindicated by the blood and treasure of a common ancestry in the war of '76, were now engaged in the attempt to do that which the British Government did, and which, by the resistance it awakened on the part of the oppressed colonists, eventuated in the establishment of our national independence. Besides, this unnatural foe was displaying a ferocity and inhumanity that far surpassed any thing ever exhibited by the British soldiery, fierce, blood-thirsty, and cruel as the "red coats" were, in the war of the Revolution. The Federal soldiery were disregarding private rights, and offering insult to the honor and sanctity of private houses. The infirmity of of old age; the helplessness of infancy and childhood; the defenceless condition of females; the pains and sufferings of the afflicted and diseased, nor the sacredness of the altars of the church, were a safeguard and protection against the violence and maltreatment of the brutal soldiery of but too many, in the invading army. In the meantime the Government at Washington was confiscating property; imprisoning men for mere opinion's sake; importing a hireling soldiery from abroad, and enacting laws that must forever stand as unrighteous and iniquitous statutes upon the journals of Congress. In this posture of affairs it is not remarkable that the young men of the land rose up in defence of mothers and sisters, whose happiness and personal safety were imperilled by the advance of the foe. Leaving all the political aspects of the subject entirely out of the question, there was enough involved on the score of personal safety, and in the claims of private homes and defenceless women, to make every father, husband, son, and brother spring to arms, and take his part in the support of a cause that, now, was fully submitted to the arbitrament of war. The sword alone, it seemed, could settle the questions at issue between the contending powers.

CHAPTER VI.

How little we know of what awaits us in the future! The clear skies of to-day, may be overcast with the clouds of to-morrow. Sunshine and shadow checker the happiest and brightest path in life. There is a tinge of sadness often commingled with the most joyous moments of our earthly existence:

> "We look before and after,
>   And sigh for what is not;
> Our sincerest laughter,
>   With some pain is fraught:
> Our sweetest songs are those
>   That tell of saddest thought."

It is well for us that we cannot penetrate the hidden future, or lift the veil that conceals the events that are to transpire in connection with our lives and fortunes in the years that lie before us in life. How many leave their homes with the certain hope and expectation of a happy return at no very distant day, who never come back again! How many who, at one stage of life, are surrounded by all the comforts, elegancies and luxuries of the happiest and most opulent earthly existence, at another are homeless and breadless, and positively destitute of the barest articles of subsistence. How many are plunged suddenly and unexpectedly from the glittering heights of fame into the lowest depths of degradation. Those who at one time are the idols and favorites of a nation, at another are the objects of a nation's scorn. Wealth, nor honor, nor intellect, nor social position, nor literary fame can furnish us a guarantee of positive exemption from painful reverses of fortune. How many a youthful hero left his home during the late war with high expectations of winning for himself a name, and making a mark in history, who, perhaps in a few weeks, or months at most, was pining in the enemy's prison at Point Lookout, at Fort Delaware, or in the Old Capitol at Washington; or who was mangled and torn by wounds inflicted in battle, and left to die on the field; or was stricken down by disease, and carried to some poorly furnished hospital to linger and die, without a friend to see him decently interred. How many a mother, who had waited long and anxiously for the return of her dear boy, only lived on under the agony of hope deferred, to receive the intelligence at last that her son was missing or dead,—no one knew his fortunes or his fate. From this line of remark, which might be pursued indefinitely, we return to the thread of our narrative, which we design to carry through these pages, linking on, here and there, by incidental digression, coincident events and other matter not entirely foreign to the subject in hand.

As we have before stated, George Harris had so far regained his health by the last of April, 1862, as to be able to return to his command, then at Yorktown. General Pickett's Brigade, to which the 19th Virginia Regiment belonged, had seen hard service for this early stage of the war. It had won for itself an enviable reputation in the battle at Manassas, at that time under command of General Cocke. It was now in front, and taking its part in the siege laid by the enemy against Yorktown. Young Harris on leaving home started for this point, hoping to be there in time, should a close engagement ensue upon that old Revolutionary ground, to share the fortunes of his company in the fight.

On his departure for camp his father accompanied him, with the design of going as far at least as Richmond; so that in the event of his relapse, should such an event occur, he might see that he received proper attention, or, if necessary, carry him back to his home. Their route was by the James river canal to Richmond. They took the packet boat at Warren, a lock-landing but a few miles distant from Col. Harris' residence, and soon were on the way down the canal. Here an opportunity was presented for calm and uninterrupted conversation between the father and his son. The excitement attendant on leaving home had subsided; and in a composed and reflective state of mind the young man spoke of the fortunes that probably awaited him in military service. He knew that he was liable at any time to fall by the hand of disease. Thousands were dying in the hospitals from pleurisy and pneumonia contracted in the camp, and from the necessary and unavoidable exposures during the winter. He knew furthermore that severe and terrific battles were imminent, and impending, and that in these, in which he expected to take a part as a private in the ranks, he would be exposed to sudden death on the field, or a lingering death in the hospital. But none of these things moved him. He was eager to reach his post of duty. He had left his home on his own motion, and at a time when others thought him rash in attempting to risk the exposures of the camp. But his mind was made up and nothing could divert him from his course. All these topics were passed in review between himself and father, as the boat was noiselessly gliding along between Warren and Scottsville. So absorbed was he in the conversation that he seemed unmindful of the crowds that thronged the boat.

The scenery on the James, along the line of the river, amid which these travellers were now passing, is attractive and beautiful; and yet on this occasion it seemed to elicit no remark, or awaken any special interest in the minds of the travellers. Rounding a wooded slope of graceful hills; gliding beneath a lofty point of beetling rocks; skirting rich and well-cultivated farms; basking in sunshine or lost in the dusky shadows of overhanging trees, all alike were powerless to divert the mind of the soldier from the one theme that seemed exclusively to occupy his thoughts.

On the arrival of the boat at Scottsville, Col. Harris met with a friend whom he expected to accompany him to Richmond on business with the government. The friend in question, however, had declined going at that time; and as they had a mutual interest to present to the consideration of the War Department, Col. Harris declined going also; and wishing to spend a longer time with his son, he persuaded him to lie over at Scottsville till the next boat— that his health was feeble—his officers were not expecting him, and that the little interval of a day or two might be spent in agreeable recreation and repose, which might contribute to his more speedy restoration to that state of bodily vigor necessary to bear up under the hardships of a soldier's life in camp. The importunities of the father for a while seemed to prevail, and the son partially consented to remain; but, as the boat again moved off, he manifested such restlessness and disappointment on account of his failure to proceed on his journey, that the friend of Col. Harris, who was looking on, said to the Colonel: "Let him go." The consent was given; and gathering up his baggage they hastened after the boat, which was not yet under full headway, overtook it, put his luggage aboard, and saw him safely on deck, and bidding him good-bye, parted with him, as it turned out, to return no more to his home and friends in Albemarle.

We can readily imagine his reflections when left alone, surrounded by strangers, and speeding his way to the army, where in a few days he might, and probably would be called on to take an active part in the impending battles, which were daily expected on the Peninsula. How entirely may one be alone, even in a busy, bustling crowd! The stranger in a strange land often feels this in the heart of a great city. Amidst its noisy marts, on its streets and thoroughfares, with the din of trade sounding in his ears, and the teeming thousands of its population around him, he may feel that *he* is *alone*. No one cares for him; no one sympathizes with him. A sense of isolation may press so heavily upon the heart, even under circumstances such as we have described, as to make one feel as lonely as if he were alone on the trackless sands of a boundless desert, or the solitary dweller on a rocky and verdureless island of the sea. Young Harris was alone on that boat amid all the stir and bustle about him. The day declined, and night came on—still he was alone. His thoughts were ever turning backward to the home and friends left behind, and then struggling to project themselves into the future that awaited him. With a rebound they came back upon himself, and he found it difficult to check the rising tear, and to suppress the involuntary sigh. He was but a youth in years and experience, and but a *private soldier* in the ranks. How should he bear up under the hardships of the approaching campaign? Who would care for him if wounded? Who would bury him if he fell? The brother to whom he could always look for sympathy and support was in his grave. Those lips were sealed in the silence of death. That generous, loving heart had ceased to beat in unison with his own. Those kind hands could no longer minister to his wants. He was alone. He felt it keenly on that first night of his severance from all that was dear to him in the circle of home.

Sad and touching is the unwritten, untold history of the *private soldier* in a great army. Too few think of it, or have thought of it. Too few regard it as worthy of note or record.

It is passed by as an idle song, and excites no more interest in the popular mind of this cold, heartless world, than the "idle tears" of childhood, or the beggar's oft-told story in the streets of a populous city.

Let us pause a moment to think of the life of the *private* in the ranks of the *Confederate* army. We speak not of the soldier by profession, who from choice or necessity has gone into the standing army for a livelihood. We speak not of the mere hireling, who has been dragged from a life of infamy into the ranks; or who has been induced to enlist for a bounty; or who has entered the army to escape the inflictions of penalties incurred by the violation of the laws; or, it may be, to save himself from sheer starvation and pinching want. We speak of the volunteers in the late Confederate service. Many of them, as we have had occasion before to remark, were young gentlemen of the highest social position in the best society. Not a few of them were mere boys and youths who had come out from the schools and colleges of the land. Most of them had been accustomed to the comforts, if not the elegancies of happy homes. But few of them had been inured to hardships or privations of any kind. Educated and refined in their sentiments, and polished in their manners, thousands upon thousands of these young men were privates in the ranks, and never rose above the position of a private or non-commissioned officer during the whole period of their continuance in service; and many of them continued from the month of April 1861, till the month of April 1865. They volunteered at the beginning of the war, and after passing through every phase of the soldier's life, received their paroles at Appomatox Court-house on the surrender of General Lee. And who is the historian that will ever attempt to chronicle and narrate the lives and fortunes of these privates in the ranks? Cold and hungry they slept, by snatches, in the open fields, without a rag of canvas to shelter them, or a blanket in which to wrap their shivering limbs. Clothed in tatters and shreds of garments, with bare feet and bare heads, and without a cracker in their haversacks, or a ration of meat in the commissary wagon, they trudged, for weary hours, night and day, on forced marches, or met the foe in the fierce and bloody battle-shock, to fight and march again. Worn down with disease, they lingered in hospitals and prisons. For long months together they lay in the muddy trenches, or burrowed in the ground like prairie-dogs, or ground-hogs, exposed to the pounding balls and exploding shells of the enemy's mortars and guns. They had no respite by furlough, and scarcely a *relief* from constant duty. Thousands sickened and died, far away from home and friends, and now sleep in graves never to be visited by those who loved them most. And yet, amid all these sufferings and hardships which no words can adequately depict, these brave and patriotic young men, without the hope or expectation of ever rising above the position of the private soldier, endured without a murmur or complaint, to the end of the war, or until their release from service was signed by Death. The artist may depict touching scenes upon the glowing canvas, and thus perpetuate the name and burial of a Latiné, or the daring and death of an occasional hero in the ranks; the poet may touch his harp and immortalize one name in a thousand; the historian may, now and then, record the deeds of a color-bearer, or the bravery of a single man in a brigade, who performed some feat of valor; but the names and deeds of the ten thousand and one of the rank and file of the Confederate soldiery will pass into the gulf of oblivion, and be forever lost to the page of history. From this digression we again return to the slender thread, which it is our purpose to weave through the entire web of this memorial sketch.

On the morning of the 19th of April 1862, we find George Harris plodding his way through the streets of Richmond, in search of information as to *where* he should find his regiment, and by what means he could get transportation to his point of destination. The streets were thronged with officers and soldiers, and army wagons moving to and fro, presenting a stirring and animating spectacle to the eye of the young soldier who had so long been absent from the field. Objects of new and unexpected interest met his gaze on every hand. Thousands of soldiers were crowding the various offices of the War Department in search of information as to the location of their different commands. By dint of perseverance George, at last, learned that he would find his regiment at Yorktown. Having obtained the desired information, he lost no time in preparing for his departure from the city.

CHAPTER VII.

LET us linger, for a little space, just at this point in our narrative, to take a view of the movements now on foot, and in process of rapid culmination. At no stage of the war were there more important and startling changes in the whole military programme, so far as Virginia was concerned, than in the month of April, and the first half of the month of May 1862. It was during this period that the design of the Federal army, then under command of General McClellan, who had succeeded McDowell, became apparent. Richmond was to be attacked by the way of James river and the Peninsula, in combination with a movement from Fredericksburg and the Potomac. Preliminary to this movement, Roanoke Island had been taken and was held by the enemy. This part of the programme—if we are right in considering it a part of it, was put in execution as early as the 10th of March. But Norfolk and Portsmouth, with the Navy Yard at Gosport, were still firmly held by the Confederates. The *Merrimac* was still prowling the waters of the Elizabeth river and Hampton Roads, to the no small discomfort and consternation of the Federal Navy that still kept at a respectful distance, hugging the walls of Fortress Monroe, and seeking shelter and protection from the formidable foe under the guns of the Fortress. Yorktown was still holding out against the enemy's guns. A powerful fleet was lying off in the bay; and from the mortars and heavy guns of the iron-clads, and other ships of war, the shot and shell, by night and day, were directed against the fortifications and other defences around the old town. But still the works were not carried, and our brave men, principally of General Longstreet's Division, and the heavy ordnance men in the forts, sought shelter in the "Bomb-proofs," and laughed at the impotent assault of the proud, triple-turreted monitors, on their bags of sand and bastions of clay. The long line of entrenchments and breastworks, stretching across the Peninsula, from Yorktown to the James, were still held by General Magruder's command, and all the gates of approach to the capitol were still bolted and barred, while strong men lay in wait and watching, and ever ready to repel the insolence of any intruder that might knock for admittance. Drury's Bluff, on the James, only nine miles below the city of Richmond, was growing into a strong and commanding fortress of defence, against the approach of the enemy's gunboats on the river. The defences around the city were constantly multiplied and extended, and were growing stronger day by day. All eyes began to turn towards Richmond. The movements of General McClellan very clearly foreshadowed his design, and the general outline of the plan of his campaign for the Spring. From official circles it began to eke out that the lower Peninsula was to be evacuated by the Confederate troops—that Norfolk was probably to be given up—that our gun-boats at Gosport were to be run up the river to Richmond —that the James river, at least as far up as Fort Powhatan, was to be left undefended, and that the Confederates were to be massed for the defence of Richmond.

From George Harris' diary we learn that he was with his regiment at Yorktown as early as the 24th of April, and was "in the ditches" on the night of the 25th, and again on the night of the 28th. Duty "*in the ditches*" around Yorktown at that time, was a bitter, burdensome, and perilous service. The following extract from McCabe's Life of General Robert E. Lee, relating to the condition of affairs at Yorktown, and on the lower Peninsula in the latter part of April 1862, will give us some idea of what it was to *go* "into the ditches," and *lie* "in the ditches" at the time referred to by young Harris. The writer says :

" The spring was wet and disagreeable, and the Peninsula, naturally marshy, was rendered nearly one bog. The troops were almost entirely without shelter, and in many instances their camps were located, unavoidably, in places where a dry spot could not be found. This caused great suffering and much sickness. The hardest work was performed by those *who held the trenches.* The proximity of the Federal army made it necessary that the whole line should be manned as fully as possible. The enemy's sharp-shooters, were, in many instances, so near that it was certain death for any one to show his head above the works. This rendered it impossible for the men in their places to stand erect, and when not actually repelling an attack, they were forced to sit down in the trenches. During all this time they were literally, not figuratively, in mud and water up to their knees. They had scarcely any food, and what was furnished them had to be passed along the trenches, from man to man, under a heavy fire of shell and musketry. They had no stimulants—not even the execrable sassafras tea with which their comrades, farther in the rear, regaled themselves in the absence of other beverages. For twenty-nine days they endured these horrible sufferings—sufferings which those who did not witness them can hardly appreciate—and yet they never murmured. I myself saw them, covered with mud, and almost famished, crawl away from the front when relieved, many of them so stiff from the effects of cold and wet, and from their cramped posture in the trenches, as to be unable to walk erect."

George Harris took his turn in the trenches, although his health was not yet fully re-established. In his diary and in his letters addressed to his friends at home he alludes to the part he took in these duties without a word of complaint; on the contrary, he seems to have taken a soldierly pride in sharing the hardest and roughest fortunes of the private in the ranks with his comrades in arms.

On the night of the 3rd, and the following day, the 4th of May, Yorktown, by the order of General Joseph E. Johnston, had been so silently and adroitly evacuated that the enemy knew nothing of the movement until the last of the troops were fairly on their retreat in the direction of Williamsburg. George Harris was detailed as one of the wagon-guard,—the train of wagons being placed in advance of the retreating army, and pushed forward toward the Chickahominy, in the direction of Richmond. He took his position and entered upon his duty; but on hearing the guns in the rear as the train pressed on through Williamsburg and beyond, and believing that his regiment was likely to be in an engagement, he went to Maj. Cabell, and earnestly begged him to grant him permission to return, and take a part in the battle. The Colonel refused; saying that he expected heavier fighting on his route than would probably fall to the lot of the regiment, and that he had no men to spare from his guard. This seems to have occurred on the evening of the 5th of May, at the time of the skirmishing and first engagement in what is known as the

Williamsburg battle. The next morning George applied to Captain Faulkner, who was still in command of the company to which George belonged, and asked to be exchanged for some other member of his company, that he might, on that day, at least, take a part in the impending fight. We are not advised as to whether the Captain granted his request or not; nor have we any memoranda which fully warrants us in saying he *was* in the fight; but, so favorably impressed was the Captain with the gallantry of young Harris that he made a note of the incident in his memorandum-book for future use.

In a certificate given by Captain Faulkner, after the death of the subject of this sketch, we find the following language in reference to the event just mentioned:

"George was detailed with the baggage-wagons at the time of the Williamsburg fight; but on hearing the guns he came to me, and requested me to exchange him, that he might be in the fight; which act I made a note of in my diary." The Captain then adds: "I was wounded in the Williamsburg battle, and left for home."

L. W. Farrar, who signs himself as Second Lieutenant, Company D, 19th Regiment Virginia Volunteers, in a certificate relating to this event in connection with others of signal courage and valor in the short soldier-life of George N. Harris, says:

"I had charge of seventy-five men who were detailed from the Regiment as wagon-guards. *George Harris was* exchanged from guard duty, at his own request, that he might go to his company, as he thought a fight would come on the next day." In the same paper he adds: "I knew George to be a gallant soldier." A friend, in a tribute of affection to this young man after his death uses the following language: "Urged by a patriotic sense of duty he wished, while at home, to return to camp, before his health would admit of it, and was only restrained from doing so, sooner than he did, by the persuasions of his friends, and the Captain of his company. The day of the battle at Williamsburg he was detailed as a wagon-guard. When he heard the sound of the guns he asked permission to go back and be in the battle, *and would not rest until he was exchanged.*"

From these somewhat conflicting accounts it would seem that his request was at last granted, but at a period too late for him to take a part in the fight. But it all goes to show the metal he was made of; and fully attests all that has been said as to his valor and gallantry as a soldier.

The Confederate army on its retreat was

pressed at various points by the Yankees, but succeeded in placing the Chickahominy between its rear and the pursuing foe. The whole of the forces that had occupied the lower Peninsula were now drawn in near Richmond, and vigorous preparations were set on foot to meet the invader; and, if necessary, repel his advances by *aggressive* movements on his lines.

The headquarters of the different commands were distributed around the city at such points as to enable the commander-in-chief to use his subordinate officers and men in such a manner as effectually to guard every avenue of access to the metropolis. But the Confederate army was too small to cope with the forces under command of McClellan. General Johnston felt the need of men, and men he must have, or the city must fall a prey to the spoiler. The Confederate Congress was slow in its movements in making provision for the increase of the army. The policy adopted was, to surrender certain points, and concentrate the whole available force in Virginia in front of McClellan's army. Accordingly on the 10th of May, Norfolk and Portsmouth were evacuated, and immediately fell into the hands of the enemy. The entire force, which for a year had lain around Norfolk, and at Sewell's Point, and the forces which more recently had occupied Portsmouth, in falling back from Roanoke Island

and Elizabeth City, all were put under orders to move in the direction of Richmond. Such gunboats and other naval craft as could ascend the James, were dispatched from the Norfolk harbor and the waters of Elizabeth river. Stealthily, by night, they crept under the guns of Newport News, and made their escape from the iron-clads and monitors lying under the shadow of the grim old Fortress at the outlet to the Bay. The noble *Merrimac* was doomed to be blown up, as it drew too much water to allow it to pass the bars in the James; and on the morning of the 11th May, when he whole of the Confederate troops had escaped from the hot pursuit of the enemy who pressed upon their heels, the match was applied; and, with a terrible explosion, the great Leviathan was torn asunder; its massive iron sheath was heaved upwards; its ponderous ribs were wrenched from their fastenings, and, settling down in the boiling waves, the circling, eddying waters closed over its sunken wreck, soon to be glided over by the keel of the fisherman's skiff, and forgotten as a thing that had been, but was not.

The news of the evacuation of Norfolk, and the blowing up of the *Merrimac* spread sadness and depression everywhere over the public mind. It was as if the knell of the Confederacy had been sounded, and the nation was summoned to the funeral.

The troops from various points which had been occupied from the commencement of the war, now being given up, began to flock to Richmond. This became the grand point of convergence. The successful repulse of the iron-clads, at Drury's Bluff, and the obstruction of the river by the sinking of several large steamers in the channel, inspired confidence in the public mind as to perfect immunity from danger in that direction. General Johnston had fully decided to defend Richmond at all hazards. His army was rapidly increasing in numbers and improving in discipline.

The month of May wore on to its close. McClellan's great army held the whole of the Peninsula, and all the country around Richmond to a point sufficiently near for his soldiers to see the spires of the city. He was confident of the capture of the prize now in sight, and almost in his grasp. But he had failed to take the gauge of the daring, the bravery, and the determination of the army that stood firmly and defiantly between him and the prize. Day by day the indignation and determination of the Confederates had been fired by the reports of outrage committed by the Yankees on females and non-combatants within their lines. Well-authenticated facts of personal violence, insult, and inhumanity reached the ears of our men, which served to inflame their valor, and give a new impulse to their patriotism. It was known to them that the cruel and heartless invaders had robbed unprotected females in New Kent, Charles City, and James City counties, of the last mouthful of subsistence; had imprisoned and cruelly beaten some of the most respectable citizens, on the merest pretexts; that noble and high-minded ladies had been outrageously insulted and maltreated; that, despite the orders of the commanding General, the subordinate officers and men had ejected helpless families from their homes; had robbed the women of their apparel; torn open their beds; smashed up their furniture; destroyed and carried off even their children's and *infants'* clothing, and in many instances had so utterly destroyed every particle of food as to reduce *mothers* to the necessity of raking up the grains of corn left upon the ground where the merciless marauders had fed their horses, to procure subsistence to keep their children from starving. These were no fictions. But for the humanity and kindness of some of the better class of Yankee officers, not a few of the good people of this section of the country would actually have perished, from the utter disregard of all the usages of civilized warfare on the part of the great mass of the foreigners and hirelings in the Yankee army.

At this juncture of affairs, General Johnston

threw a portion of his forces against the left of McClellan's army then occupying the right bank of the Chickahominy; and here, on the 31st day of May, was fought that fierce and terrific battle, known as the battle of the Seven Pines. Here again we meet with our young soldier, but reserve more special reference to the part he took in this fight for the next chapter.

CHAPTER VIII.

The battle of Seven Pines was one of the severest and most hotly contested of all the battles of the war. The fighting was desperate, and the mortality fearful. At the commencement of this fierce and very bloody conflict, Col. Strange, who was in command of the 19th Regiment, in Pickett's Brigade, placed a parcel of deserters in the rear of the line of battle, under guard, as a punishment for their pusillanimity and dastardly conduct. George Harris was detailed as one of the guard to take charge of this band of deserters. General Pickett seeing the exposed condition of the guard, ordered them to retire to a place of greater safety. While the battle was raging at its height, George took one of the guard, and one of the deserters who volunteered for the adventure, and made a dash upon a squad of Yankees, and directly brought in ten prisoners. The deserter who took a part in this bold and hazardous act, was deemed to have merited exemption from further punishment, and was accordingly discharged and returned to his company.

Captain Faulkner, in a long certificate in which he testifies to the undaunted courage and daring of George Harris as a member of his company, and in which he recounts a number of his bold and heroic acts as we shall further see at a later stage of this narration—a certificate from which we have already made extracts, says, with regard to the deed just recorded:

"When I returned to my company [having been wounded on the retreat from Williamsburg] I was credibly informed that at the battle of Seven Pines, George Harris was detailed to take charge of some deserters. To punish them they were placed in the rear of the line. General Pickett ordered them to fall back to a place of safety. Having complied with the order, George took one prisoner and one soldier, and went on the battle-field and brought in ten prisoners."

The certificate from which this extract is made, as before stated, is signed by Captain Faulkner in regular form. When this battle was over, in which Pickett's Brigade took an active and conspicuous part, both on the afternoon of the 31st of May, and then again, with but little support, on the morning of June the 1st, and in which our troops suffered such terrible slaughter, while storming the powerful forts and other defences of the enemy—when the conflict was over, no one displayed more kindness and attention to the wounded and dying on the battle-field, so far as it was in his power, than George Harris. He assisted in loading the ambulances with the mangled bodies of his comrades who had fallen. He was as tender and sympathetic as he was manly and brave; and he permitted no opportunity to pass unimproved that presented an occasion for him to render an act of kind attention to a suffering fellow-soldier.

During the few weeks that intervened between the battle of Seven Pines and the renewal of active hostilities in the Seven Days' fighting around Richmond, a great deal of sickness prevailed in camp among the soldiers. Many remained in their tents and in the temporary field-hospitals, because of the crowded condition of the hospitals in the city, to which the wounded had been carried after the fearful carnage of Seven Pines. George Harris gave himself up, so far as his other duties would permit, to the nursing of the sick in camp. He was assiduous and untiring in his attentions, and seemed never to grow weary of his work.

As we have said, the hospitals and private houses of Richmond were crowded with the wounded from the battle-field of Seven Pines. The havoc of that engagement was really awful and appalling. Thousands were carried into the city, who were too badly mangled to be removed to more remote points; and thousands more, on furlough, were permitted to return to their friends at home for nursing, care and attention. The 11th Regiment of Virginia volunteers, commanded by Colonel Garland, in which was the "*Home Guards*," and "Rifle Grays," from Lynchburg, suffered fearfully in this fight. A number of young men in these companies were killed, and temporarily interred on the field; while many more were severely wounded. We well remember the sad day on which the remains of some five or six of these brave and noble men—the flower of the Hill City—having been disinterred, were brought to Lynchburg. The whole city turned out to attend the funeral solemnities, and to follow them to Spring Hill Cemetery for final burial, in a lot specially set apart for the interment of the soldiers of Lynchburg who fell in battle. It was a touching spectacle. And to this day many homes are dark and disconsolate from the results of *that* battle; which, while it was successful in driving the enemy from the field with almost unprecedented slaughter for the time it lasted, nevertheless left more of our own men dead and wounded than has ever been reported to have fallen to the lot of the enemy.

The scenes presented in Richmond during the first few weeks immediately following the battle of Seven Pines, were as beautiful, in their moral aspects, as they were painful and revolting in a physical point of view. Never was there a greater and more spontaneous exhibition of patriotism, hospitality and generous kindness displayed by any people than was manifested, on every hand, by the citizens on this occasion. Every door was thrown open to the wounded soldiers. Every woman and little girl became a nurse and a watcher by the bed-side of the sufferer. Flowers were gathered from every garden, and woven into beautiful bouquets to ornament the little tables in the hospitals, and regale the inmates with their fragrance. Sweet-faced little girls, clad in white, sat by many a couch and fanned the fevered and aching brow of the soldier, who lay with broken limbs and mangled body upon his restless pillow. Nothing that private hospitality could afford from larder or wardrobe was thought to be too good for the men who had bared their breasts in defence of the city. In these kind and tender attentions bestowed upon the men who were far away from their homes and kindred, the ladies of Richmond won for themselves a name that will be remembered with gratitude and thankfulness, while the last man lives who was a recipient of favors from their beneficent hands.

During the interval of which we now speak George Harris received a visit in camp from his father, who bore him tidings and greetings from home. The patriotic old gentleman shared the fare of his son in his mess, and in his tent, taking care, in the meantime, to contribute something to the soldiers' repast, not dealt out in the usual rations. The well-filled box, prepared by the mother's hand, opened its more inviting provisions to George's eye, and these he shared with his mess-mates with that generous unselfishness for which he was so distinguished. At that time he had a sick cousin in camp, who was very ill, and growing worse from day to day. In his behalf he felt the liveliest interest, and did all he could, *as a private*, in conjunction with his father, to obtain a sick furlough for him, that he might return to his home for nursing and recovery. This sick relative was a member of the 56th Virginia regiment. George, hearing of his illness, sought him out, and found him in an open log hut, wounded and suffering with measles. His condition was perilous, and without proper attention he must die. George went to Captain Lobbin, who had command of the sick man's company—represented the case, and readily obtained his consent for removal by furlough. Doctor Luck, the assistant Physician to the regiment, granted his permission and recommendation. Governor Smith, who was Colonel of his regiment, also consented and gave his recommendation. At another point the application met with a stern and rude rebuff. That night it rained heavily. The hut was damp and chilly. The sick man became worse—was carried to a hospital in Richmond. In a few days a furlough was obtained for him, but it was too late. He was put on the packet-boat to go to Albemarle, but that night he died, and was carried home a corpse. This was the history of very many *privates* in the Confederate service. We pass it by without further remark or comment, other than to say, that this young man had merited, by his valor, a better fortune and a more considerate attention than he received. In the battle of Seven Pines he fought bravely. A fellow-soldier by his side, in the fight, was shot dead, and in falling knocked this young man down and fell on him. On rising to his feet a ball struck him on the breast, but fortunately was turned aside by a metal button—saving his life. He was wounded, but not disabled. Still he held his position in the ranks. The color-bearer of his regiment was shot down. No one volunteered to take it up; when this young man sprang forward and seized the shattered staff, and bore its tattered folds aloft and in triumph through the fight. The name of this young man was HENRY T. HARRIS. He was a *private* in the ranks, and the future historian of our battles will, perhaps, never hear his name; we take pride in giving it a place in this unpretending sketch.

George's father would have been pleased to carry his son home with him on a short furlough, on the occasion of this visit to the camp, but George was unwilling to make application, and said that he would not leave the army at *that* time, when the service of every man who could shoulder his musket was in demand, even if his father was to obtain a furlough for him. He was too true a soldier to allow himself to be out of the way of duty or danger when it came to the lot of his regiment. He must take his part in every engagement, and faithfully perform his full portion of duty in the regular round of service falling to his company. We shall meet this brave youth again at another point in his history.

Movements were now on foot for impending battles. Troops by the thousand had been gathering around Richmond daily, from all parts of the Confederacy. General Johnston having been wounded in the battle of Seven

Pines, General Lee was now in command of the army. Stirring events were almost hourly transpiring in the Valley of Virginia. That thunderbolt of war, General Stonewall Jackson, had been, and then was, playing terrible havoc with the Union forces under command of Fremont, Banks, and Shields. McClellan was pushing his lines nearer and nearer to Richmond. Expectation was on tiptoe, and yet no blow was struck of an important character in the vicinity of the capital. General Lee was cautiously laying his plans to countervail the movements of the no less cautious McClellan. They were watching each other with vigilance. But a great, decisive battle, was near at hand. McClellan had pushed the right wing of his army as far as Hanover Court House. He was now holding a long line, occupying both banks of the Chickahominy, and sweeping far round the city. His army was known to be powerful in numbers, well-provisioned, thoroughly equipped, and well disciplined for the time they had been in service. Lee's army was, numerically, far smaller than McClellan's; but the morale of his men was good, and their bravery unquestioned, and unquestionable. In this condition of affairs about Richmond, and with General Jackson stealthily moving down the Central Railroad, to be ready at the commencement of an offensive attack, now determined on by General Lee, to strike the enemy's right on the flank and in the. rear, we wait for the developments of to-morrow.

CHAPTER IX.

The storm, which had been gathering for so long a time around the capital, was just now ready to break in all its violence and fury. The fitful glare of the lightning had been seen, and the distant thunder had now and then been heard, foretokening the coming storm; but now the hush and lull that struck every one on the morning of the 26th June, 1862, awakened the apprehension that the long-expected hour was at hand.

On the afternoon of that memorable 26th of June, as the sun was bending to the horizon, General A. P. Hill's division moved down the Mechanicsville turnpike towards "Meadow Bridges." The Fortieth Virginia Regiment, followed by Pegram's Battery, crossed the Bridges, drove in the enemy's pickets, and pressed rapidly on towards Mechanicsville. The line of battle was formed, and ere the going down of the sun on that day, what is known as the "Seven Days' Battle" around Richmond was fairly inaugurated. The enemy was met in considerable force in this first engagement, and the advance of the Confederate troops was hotly contested. The fight was kept up with severity until nine o'clock at night, when the battle ceased to rage; and, while the advancing troops slept on their arms, the enemy, under cover of the night, fell back in the direction of Coal Harbor and Gaines' Mill. The dawn of Friday morning, 27th of June, found a large portion of General Lee's great army in motion. General Longstreet's whole division had crossed the Chickahominy, from the south to the north side, and moved, in its different brigades, down the river, and towards Coal Harbor. In the meantime, General Jackson, who had left Ashland on the previous day (the 26th) with his forces, had stealthily moved down the right bank of the Pamunkey, gradually bearing in towards the Chickahominy, and was now hovering on the rear of the extreme right of McClellan's army. The day was again declining. Jackson's guns were heard at Coal Harbor, announcing the commencement of the attack upon the enemy's lines. This was the signal for a general dash upon the Yankee forces; and, in a very short time, the engagement extended for miles along the line of the strongholds of McClellan's army on the north side of the Chickahominy. If, on the evening before, when A. P. Hill's division engaged a mere handful, comparatively, of the enemy's forces, the whole of Richmond turned out upon the hills and fields surrounding the city to witness what might be heard and seen of the *opening* of the great battle, and remained out-doors till a late hour to hear the latest tidings from the field, and to witness the last flash from the guns that broke the gloom of night in this fierce and deadly conflict, what must have been the extent and intensity of the interest and excitement that now pervaded every patriotic bosom within the hearing of the awful and terrific fight that continued to rage with unabated severity through the long hours of a long afternoon, of a long summer's day, and only ceased with the gathering darkness that closed in that bloody 27th of June!

Here our heroic young soldier emerges again from the great mass of the army, and stands out in his individuality. Where so many are brave, and daring, and chivalrous, and where so many seem to share equally in the performance of noble and decisive deeds, it seems almost invidious to single out any particular *one*, and award to him a praise to which, it may be, many others are equally entitled with himself.

In stating what we are now about to recount as connected with the part taken by *George N. Harris* in the storming of one of the strongest points in the enemy's line of defences on the evening of the 27th, we do not intend thereby to detract in the least from the gallantry and valor of others, nor to make a hero of *one* to the disparagement of his fellows. Our object is simply to do justice to the conspicuous and valorous part enacted by the subject of this memorial sketch in the bloody tragedy that resulted in the capture of the enemy's strongest and most formidable position at Gaines' Mill.

In all the battles of the war there was not a more desperate and murderous fight than that which occurred at Gaines' Mill on the 27th June, 1862. The slaughter of the Confederates in their repeated assaults upon the powerful defences of the Yankees was perfectly appalling. Time and again repulsed, they as often renewed the assaults; and, while thousands fell, the ranks were instantly refilled, and the bold, brave, dauntless men rushed forward over the heaps of the wounded, dead, and dying, and never gave up the struggle until the last stronghold was carried and the enemy was compelled to commence a humiliating and inglorious retreat that carried him over the Chickahominy, across the swamps, and through the thickets to the banks of the James, from which point the grand invading army of the Potomac took its departure from the Peninsula, in the abandonment of the long-cherished hope and expectation of capturing Richmond in the spring and summer campaign of 1862.

The *turning point* in the fortunes and career of McClellan's grand army was at Gaines' Mill. The dislodgment of the Yankees from their apparently impregnable position *at this point*, rendered it necessary for McClellan to make good his retreat to the banks of the James river, or to suffer the capture, or utter annihilation of his army. Lee's forces were so distributed as to cut him off from his base of supplies on the Pamunkey, and the only alternative left him was retreat, or inevitable discomfiture.

Let us now, with these facts before us, look for a little while at the turning point, at Gaines' Mill; for this confessedly was the turning point. The capture of the enemy's strongest point in that formidable line of entrenched fortifications, put the key of the situation in the hands of the commanding General of the Confederate troops, and ensured to him the historic renown, through the ages to come, of having, at least, defeated a great army, under the command of a skilful General, at the last point of a succession of advances that seemed to place the coveted prize in the hands of the invaders whenever it should be their pleasure to strike the blow and claim the boon.

General Jackson, in his official report of the battle at Gaines' Mill, alludes in the following terms to the charge of Hood's and Law's Brigades of Whiting's Division, in which the most formidable garrison on the strongly fortified crest of the range of hills held by the Yankees was carried and held:

"Dashing on with unfaltering step, in the face of the murderous discharge of canister and musketry, General Hood and Colonel Law, at the head of their respective brigades, rushed to the charge with a yell. Moving down a precipitous ravine, leaping ditch and stream, clambering up a difficult ascent, and exposed to an incessant and deadly fire from the entrenchments, these brave and determined men pressed forward, driving the enemy from his well-selected and fortified position. In the charge, in which upwards of a thousand men fell, killed and wounded, and in which fourteen pieces of artillery, and nearly a regiment of men were captured, the *Fourth* Texas, under the lead of General Hood, was the *first* to pierce the stronghold, and seize the guns."

Pollard, in his history of "The First Year of the War," speaking of this battle, and of its crowning event, to which the extract from General Jackson's official report refers, says:

"General A. P. Hill made the first assault upon the lines of the enemy's entrenchments near Gaines' Mill. A fierce struggle had ensued between his Division and the garrison of the line of defence. Repeated charges were made by Hill's troops, but the formidable character of the works, and murderous volleys of grape and canister from the artillery covering them, kept our troops in check. It was past four o'clock when *Pickett's* Brigade from Longstreet's Division, came to Hill's support. *Pickett's Regiment fought with the most determined valor.* At last Whiting's Division, composed of the "Old Third" and Texan Brigades, advanced at a double quick, charged *the batteries*, and drove the enemy from his strong line of defence."

In this last successful charge, George N. Harris took a singularly active and conspicuous part for a private soldier in the ranks.

It appears from a number of certificates now before the writer, that the 19th Regiment of Pickett's Division was ordered to charge a battery of the enemy that was holding a strong position in the enemy's line of defences. George Harris led the van. "For some reason," as stated by an eye-witness and actor in the charge, "the regiment failed to advance, or at least to carry out the orders into full execution,—perhaps were ordered to halt or fall back. But, in any event, George Harris and one other member of his company pressed forward, and became separated from their command. Just at this point a Texas regiment of Whiting's Division was found pressing forward in a desperate charge on the battery in question. George Harris took the lead in this regiment. Most of the officers had been wounded, and had fallen in the charge. George Harris assumed command; or, in other words, his valor and gallantry placed him at the head of the advancing charge. He led the charge with hat in hand, shouting to the men to come on. He ordered the surrender of the battery, and was the first man to put his hands upon the guns, and turn them on the enemy."

As this was really the crowning act of George's soldier-life, we will bring it out a little more prominently and conspicuously in this sketch.

W. F. Clarke, Sergeant in Company D. of the 19th Regiment, gives the following certificate, dated March 2d, 1863.

"As an eye-witness, I hereby certify that George N. Harris acted with conspicuous valor in the battle at Gaines' Mill, June 27th, 1862. I saw him when firing at the Yankees, clear the front of his line, take deliberate aim, fire and fall back to load, and that too when our own men in the rear line were actually killing our men in front. He was in front in a charge, and I heard him say, (and others confirmed it,) that he ordered the greater portion of the Third Federal Regiment to surrender, but they fired into our men, when he ordered our men to return the fire, whereupon they surrendered. He was the first man to put his hand upon the battery captured in the charge."

(Signed),

"W. F. CLARK, Sergeant Co. D, 19th Reg'mt Va. Vols."

Captain J. Faulkner, who had command of this company, in the long certificate from which we have already made some extracts, says, with regard to the particular event now under notice:

"At Gaines' Mill he (George Harris) led off in two separate charges, and was the first to put his hands on the captured battery. I have seen Sergeant Clarke's certificate, and fully endorse it."

L. W. Farrar, who signs himself Second Lieutenant, Co. D, 19th Regiment Virginia Volunteers, says:

"I was wounded in the battle at Gaines' Mill, early in the fight. As far as I went *George N. Harris was ever in front.* I know him to be a gallant soldier, and do cheerfully endorse the above. * * * * I also endorse Sergeant Clarke's certificate, knowing him to be a man of truth and high respectability."

In further attestation of the valor and daring of young Harris, we subjoin the certificate of

C. Scott, Jr., who was a member of the same company, and who was an eye-witness of the part taken by Harris in the final charge, on the occasion referred to, which turned the fortunes of McClellan's grand army on the Chickahominy.

"I certify that George N. Harris was with us in the fight on Friday, 27th June, 1862, at Gaines' Mill, and acted with great gallantry. At one time during this battle our regiment (the 19th Va.) was ordered to charge one of the batteries of the enemy. In this charge *he* gallantly led the van. For some reason the regiment did not reach the battery, either because they were ordered to halt or fall back. I did not hear the order, neither did Harris; but he continued the charge, and when I reached the battery he was there. About the same time a Texas regiment came up. At this time another battery of the enemy commenced firing on us, and being thus separated from *our* regiment (the 19th), we joined the Texans in a second charge upon this battery which was also taken. In every conflict he exhibited the most heroic courage, seeming utterly regardless of his personal safety."

(Signed), "C. SCOTT, JR."

From the foregoing statements it is placed beyond a doubt, that George Harris displayed signal valor, and won for himself imperishable

honors at the battle of Gaines' Mill. The
same deeds which he performed as a private in
the ranks, had they been performed by an
officer of rank would have secured for him
not only promotion, but would have insured
for him an honorable record upon the page of
history.

The following is substantially a summary
statement of this characteristic act of George
Harris' life. A. P. Hill's division had brought
on the engagement on the 27th of June, at
Gaines' Mill. The men had made frequent
gallant charges, but were as often repulsed,
and forced to fall back. About four o'clock in
the afternoon Pickett's invincible brigade was
called to his aid. It was in this first onset of
Pickett's men that George Harris was seen
clearing the smoke and dust of the battle strife
—firing deliberately, and falling back to the
line to load. Finally the order was given to
charge, and take the battery in front of Pickett's Brigade. The 19th Regiment moved forward. All the officers of the regiment then
on the field, had been wounded in the last
hour. George Harris led in the charge, as
we have before described. He moved at the
top of his speed, without looking behind, and
cried, "Come on boys." Just then, accord-
ing to the account we are following, the first
Texan, and the Fourth South Carolina rush-

ed forward from each side, and cut off the *Nineteenth* Virginia. It was this movement that placed our young hero in front of the charging column. At a suitable distance he ordered the battery to surrender. They replied by firing on the advancing line. At the command of George Harris the fire was returned, and immediately the battery surrendered, supported by two hundred and fifty men. The impetuous advance of our troops so confused and intimidated the enemy that their fire was comparatively harmless in the last assault, and the bold hand of George Harris turned the captured battery with deadly effect upon the defeated and retiring foe.

In all these exposed positions Harris escaped unharmed. A wonderful providence preserved him amid peril and danger. Night closed this fearful contest. The Confederates had carried the day, but at the sacrifice of many thousands of noble men. And here, for the present, we leave Harris, and his comrade Scott, with the Texas regiment.

CHAPTER X.

THE retreat of McClellan was marked by distinguished skill and generalship. He succeeded in eluding the vigilant eye of General Lee, and in making good his movements in the direction of James river. Being cut off from his principal sources of supply on the Pamunkey, and York rivers, and losing the control of the Central Railroad, the only alternative left him was, to reach the James river, and retreat down the Peninsula, or to suffer an inglorious defeat in the capture of his whole army. The alternative was promptly accepted by the cautious McClellan, and the retreat was conducted, in all its parts, with a skill that must ever reflect the very highest credit upon the military leadership of this general, who has come in for so large a share of criticism and abuse from the Yankee nation.

The fierce contest at Gaines' Mill, as we have seen, turned the tide of battle in favor of the Confederates. General Lee was not slow to discover that McClellan was retreating, but the difficulty was to detect by what route, or line of march he purposed effecting his escape from the swamps of the Chickahominy, and reaching a point of safety for his army. General Lee was on the alert, and yet, on the Monday following the fight at Gaines' Mill on Friday, we find McClellan, after a few skirmishes here and there, between his rearguard and the pursuing foe emerging from White Oak swamp, with his men and army wagons, all in pretty good trim, and pressing on in the direction of Harrison's Landing on James river. But, on debouching from the swamp, the Yankee general, with all his shrewdness, found himself confronted by General Longstreet's whole division, supported by General Hill's division of six brigades. And here, on the afternoon of Monday, June 30th, was fought the battle of Frazier's Farm. And a terrible battle it was, but it resulted in the triumph of the Confederate arms. Pickett's Brigade was again in the thick of this fight. The slaughter was immense on both sides. As the Yankees were driven back in the contest the ground was found literally covered with their men. Night came on, and hung its gloomy curtains over the battle field. The groans of the wounded were heard in every direction during the hours of that sad night. The wearied and worn-out soldiers, who had been constantly in pursuit of the retreating enemy for several days and nights in succession, were not able, from sheer exhaustion, to explore the field that night in search of their missing comrades. Falling down upon their arms, they slept away the passing hours, surrounded by the wounded, the dead, and the dying.

From the date of this battle on Frazier's Farm, June 30th, 1862, George A. Harris disappears from the ranks. But where is he? What have been the fortunes of the brave young man? Is he among the dead, who lie so quietly upon the damp earth, sleeping the last sleep of the soldier? or, is he writhing in pain, with shattered limbs, and bullet-torn muscles, unable to help himself, and crying to some member of the ambulance committee, who is seen with torch in hand, peering into the faces of the dead, or picking up the wounded on the field, to come to his relief? or, is he a prisoner? It would seem that no one was present when the inquiry was made as to the fortunes of young Harris, who could give any satisfactory answer; and, in the excitement and confusion attendant on this stage of the seven days fighting around Richmond, many were lost sight of, whose absence from roll-call scarcely awakened a thought in the minds of those who responded to their names. The Confederate army was becoming disorganized. Some of its strongest brigades were so decimated as scarcely to be able to present a line equal to an ordinary company. Thousands had fallen out of the ranks from exhaustion. They were scattered through the woods, in the swamps, and over the fields, and the wonder is that a sufficient number could be brought into line of battle, to make any thing like a respectable fight at Malvern Hills, where the Yankees made their last stand, and from which point they soon found refuge and safety under their gunboats on James river.

As we have said, George Harris, in whose history and fortunes we are more particularly interested in this narrative, was missing after the battle on Frazier's farm. There was *one* who knew his fate, but *he* seems not to have been in a position to communicate with any of George's friends, so as to relieve their minds from the painful suspense in which they had been thrown by the uncertainty which hung around his fortunes in that bloody battle.

On Tuesday July 1st, the day after the battle on Frazier's farm, Col. Harris left his home in Albemarle for the purpose of visiting the army that he might learn something of the incidents connected with the life of his son during the recent battles, in which so many had fallen. On his way down the James-river canal, he met the upward bound boat, on which he found three of his son's comrades, members of the same company, who had been wounded, and were now returning home on furlough. On hailing them and inquiring after his son, they congratulated him on George's safety, stating that he had passed through all the battles, taking an active part whenever his regiment was engaged, and that he had sustained no damage. On the arrival of the boat in Richmond on Wednesday morning, the Colonel was met by other friends who assured him of George's safety and well-being. But, on reaching the hotel where he put up for a little while before leaving for the camp below the city, he was told by some persons who seemed to have correct and direct intelligence upon the subject, that George was seen to fall at Frazier's farm, or, that in any event, he had been missing since that fight. This intelligence was received with some degree of doubt as to its correctness, for several reasons. In the first place a number of George Harris' comrades had given the direct and positive information that he was safe. Then it seemed improbable that he had been seen to fall, since no one pretended to say his body had been discovered on the field. More than that, it was known that George's mess-mate, James Harris, had fallen, and the father hoped that it was he, and not George, who had been seen to fall in the fight. But, notwithstanding all these facts and circumstances which seemed so forcibly to contradict the report of the death of George Harris, his father's fears were aroused. He had the painful apprehension that it might be so; and, with a heavy heart he proceeded to the regimental camp about four miles below Richmond, for the purpose of learning all that might be known of George's fate and condition. On reaching the camp where he had visited his son only some two weeks previous, he found it deserted. Scarcely a trace was left behind. Army and artillery wagons had rolled over every inch of the ground. Thousands and tens of thousands of soldiers in their march had trampled down every living thing. Fences were pulled down; fields were down-trodden; lonely chimneys, and charred ruins told where the hospitable and happy homes of the wealthy farmers of the country had stood; an air of utter desolation reigned on every hand, and scarcely a solitary landmark was left to guide the traveller over this almost interminable waste. The rain was descending in torrents, and yet the father, in pursuit of his soldier boy, was not to be deterred by swollen streams, and muddy roads. On foot he started for Malvern Hill, hearing that probably the 19th regiment would be found in that vicinity. That night found him amid the stirring and exciting scenes of the final withdrawal of McClellan's forces from the field of conflict. He failed to come up with the regiment for which he was so anxiously looking; but, from various sources he learned that the prevailing impression was that George had ventured too far in advance of his company on the day of the battle when he was last seen, and that he had been captured, and was most probably a prisoner in the hands of the enemy. Colonel Harris slept that night on the battle field of Malvern Hill, and the next morning retraced his steps to Frazier's farm, where his son had last been seen. Here amongst the still unburied dead, he commenced a diligent search for the body of his son; but, after spending several hours in this painful employment, without discovering any trace of his lost boy, he abandoned further search, hoping that he might be a captive in the hands of the Yankees. No satisfactory information could be obtained from any quarter as to his probable condition, and the father left the field, and returned to Richmond—thence to his home in Albemarle, without being able to bear to his family any reliable intelligence as to the fortunes of George. Vague reports, which could be traced to no responsible author, were almost daily reaching the family in their mountain home, to the effect that George Harris was dead. These rumors intensified the pain of the suspense. Nothing definite could be learned from any person. Three weeks of unspeakable anxiety had passed away, when full reports from the different regiments, giving the names of all that had been taken prisoners from the different companies, were published. The report from the 19th regiment, and especially from company D of that regiment, was eagerly examined; but nothing was said of George Harris.

This determined Col. Harris to make another visit to the army with the hope of learning something definite with regard to his son's disappearance from the ranks. The suspense was too bitter. He must find relief. The cloud that invested this mystery must be dissipated. He accordingly left again for the army, resolved never to rest until the mystery was solved.

CHAPTER XI.

FRIENDLY reader, did you ever search a battle-field for the body of a missing son, brother, friend? Did you ever ramble among the dead, lying on the bare earth, just as they had fallen in the deadly conflict, eagerly scanning every form, and feature, with the hope of recognizing the missing one? What a spectacle was presented to your prying eye, and inquiring gaze! One there had fallen on his face; another yonder lay on his back, with his glaring eyes fixed in their sockets, and his teeth firmly clenched as they were set in the death-agony. Beneath that shrub lies another, with his hands clasped above his head, and his eyelids closed in the sleep of death. Wounded, he dragged himself to the shelter of the stunted bush, and stretched himself out to die. Lying yonder is a flaxen-haired boy. Scarcely seventeen summers have passed over him. His cheek is smooth, and once was fair. His hand—delicate as a girl's, grasps firmly still the musket that was levelled in its deadly aim when he fell. Here lies a stalwart form, with bronzed cheek, firmly-knit joints, hard and horny hands, and unkempt hair. He came from his humble home among the hills, and fought and fell in freedom's cause. Just there is still another. His locks are gray; his brow is furrowed with time's rude ploughshare—almost an *old* man, he seems to be. Prompted by a fervid patriotism he left his wife and daughters in the dear old homestead, among the magnolias of the South, and with his sons volunteered in the service of his country; and now here he lies, till stranger-hands shall scoop out his shallow grave and throw a few shovels of earth upon his uncoffined body. What a spectacle! Young and middle aged, and even the old, are mingled promiscuously on the field where the storm of lead and iron, mixed with fire and sulphurous fumes, dealt death and carnage on the right and left. Amid a scene like this, with the earth torn and rent beneath your feet by the wheels of artillery wagons, or ploughed by shot and shell; with the trees and shrubs around you scarred and riddled by grape and canister and minie balls ; with the debris of battle scattered in every direction, and the unburied bodies of the slain meeting the eye far and near, over as wide a space as the vision could traverse and survey—amid a scene like this, did you ever search for a missing one that you loved? How scrutinizingly you peered into that upturned face! How carefully and tenderly you turned over that manly form, not knowing but that you might recognize the object of your search in the frigid features that were to meet your eye on turning up the face that was buried in the dust! With what an eye of anxious inquiry did you examine even the torn limb, and other fragments of the mangled body, where the face and other features were destroyed, thinking that, possibly, by some well-remembered scar, or by some peculiar turn of joint or form you might catch some trace that would reveal to your breaking heart the fortunes of the missing one. Where recognition was rendered impossible by the destruction of the body, you even examined the shreds and tatters of the garments worn, with the hope, if the object of your pursuit had really fallen on the field, that you might detect the initials of the name, wrought by a mother's hand, or discover some part of a garment prepared by a sister's love, or find some stitch, or button that might give the clue to the desired discovery.

How sad and depressing, after such a search as that described above, to leave the field without making any discovery that leads to a satisfactory conclusion! Colonel Harris, as we have seen in the foregoing chapter, had utterly failed in his efforts to learn any thing certain as to the fate of his son. For three long weeks, the vulture-beak of doubt and suspense had been digging into the hearts of this suffering family. The days and nights had dragged heavily along, as they anxiously waited for further, and more satisfactory tidings from the missing one.

The father, as we have seen, had left his sorrowing and unhappy family again to visit the army, for the purpose of making further inquiry and investigation in relation to the disappearance of his son. By the same route over which he had so frequently travelled, on his visits to the army, he reached Richmond;

but, without tarrying longer than was necessary to ascertain where he might find the 19th Regiment, he hastened on to the camp. Here all his doubts were dissipated, and he was wakened up to the solemn realization of the fact that George was *dead*—not a prisoner in the hands of the enemy, but the tenant of a soldier's grave on the field where he fell. *James Christian*, of Amherst county, who was in the same regiment with George Harris, was in the skirmish line with George on the day of the battle on Frazier's farm. He gave the following account of what transpired in connection with George's death. The skirmishing had been going on all the morning, but, for the most part in the woods, among the pines and tangled undergrowth. On emerging from the pines into an open, sedgy sort of a plain, the first volley from the enemy's line was poured into the line of skirmishers. A young man by the name of Wingfield received a wound, and fell. He called to James Christian for assistance; and, on turning to him, Christian saw that George Harris too had fallen—not wounded merely, but shot through the heart. A bullet had struck him while he was in the excitement of bringing on an engagement; and, without a word—without a groan, or a struggle, his career was terminated, and his spirit dislodged from its tenement of clay. What a transition! How sudden! He who had displayed such valor, and who had passed through all the previous perils and dangers to which he had been exposed, without a scratch, was now cut down in an instant. His dreams of ambition were extinguished in a moment of time. "What is your life?" inquires an inspired writer. To his own inquiry he gives the answer " It is even a vapor, that appeareth for a little while, and then vanisheth away."

On the receipt of this intelligence by Col. Harris of the death of his son, he was further informed by young Christian that he had such a distinct and vivid recollection of the spot where George fell, that he could conduct him to the grave. Whereupon two or three other soldiers besides James Christian were detailed to accompany Col. Harris in search of his son's remains. On reaching the point where the skirmish line emerged from the pines on the day of the battle on Frazier's farm, young Christian pointed to the spot where George fell; and then to the little mound that had been raised over the body of his comrade in arms. In further attestation of the identification of the fact of his death and interment at that spot, he pointed to the felt hat hanging on a bush near the grave, which, on examination, Col. Harris found to be the one he had given his son on his last visit to the camp, just before the beginning of the Seven Days' fight around Richmond.

The spot being fully identified, so as to prevent any future mistake, the father returned to the camp, and thence to his home in Albemarle, proposing, in the course of a few days, to return for the remains of his son.

While in camp, on the occasion of the visit just alluded to, Col. Harris had the gratification to hear the highest eulogies bestowed upon his son by his comrades in arms. They spoke in unmeasured terms of his gallantry, daring, and bravery as a soldier; of his urbanity and courteous bearing as a gentleman; of his generosity, kindness, and fidelity as a friend, and of his high-toned morality as a Christian. Every thing was said in his praise. The soldiers seemed to vie with each other in the bestowment of compliment and commendation upon him. Every one deeply regretted his loss. This, of course, was gratifying to the bereaved and disconsolate father, but nothing could pluck the deep-seated grief from his heart. It was a touching spectacle to see that devoted father, now more than threescore years of age, surrounded by the young men who had been the associates and companions of his lost boy, and each one endeavoring by the expression of sympathy with the bereaved to alleviate the bitterness of the sad and sorrowful hour through which he was passing. The occasion served to strengthen the attachment of Col. Harris to the young men of his son's company ; but, especially, to bind him to JAMES CHRISTIAN, the young man who had been the instrument of saving the grave of George Harris from becoming irrecoverably lost. But for his thoughtful attention in noting the place of interment, and so marking it in his reccollection, even in the battle strife, as to distinguish it from the surrounding graves, the parents of this brave and noble young man would have been doomed to the life-long sorrow of not even knowing where his body rested. Indeed, but for the considerate attentions of James Christian, the parents and friends of George Harris might never have known how, and under what circumstances he disappeared from his accustomed place in the ranks. Thousands of privates in the ranks, who really distinguished themselves by valorous deeds, fell at last—if not without a grave, at least without a stone or piece of plank even to mark the spot of interment. Pits were dug, and hundreds of these brave and heroic fellows, who died battling for the Confederate cause, were tumbled in together. Memorial associations cannot rescue these graves—if graves they may be called, from utter and irrecoverable loss and oblivion. No mother's footsteps can ever visit the spot where her soldier-boy sleeps, for the place is unknown. No sister's hand can lay the wreath of flowers, as a tribute of affection, upon his tomb, for he was cast with scores of others into the trench, and no one knows where that trench was dug. The kindness and forethought of James Christian rescued the grave of George Harris, and rendered it possible for parental love to manifest itself in the removal of the remains, and giving them a Christian burial in the old family burying-ground, where his kindred for three or four generations slumbered peacefully in their turf-sodded graves.

How sad to think that this young man, *Christian*, who was so thoughtful of others, and who, by his generosity and nobleness of nature, had bound so many hearts to him, fell at last in the battle of Boonsboro, and, if buried at all, no one knows the place of his interment to this day. What a pity that the grave of such a *man*, and such a soldier, should be lost. He deserves a monument of marble, and an epitaph in characters of gold, to tell to the passing generations, in the lapse of time, the name and virtues of an unselfish and gallant hero, who was as tender as he was brave; and who, amid all the hardening and demoralizing influences of the camp and the field, carried with him to the last battle in which he fought and fell, a nature as genial, generous, and guileless, as it was patriotic, valorous, and courageous. Nothing could daunt, or intimidate him in battle; nothing could make him forget the offices of friendship, and the missions of mercy when the battle was over. A brave soldier, a faithful friend, and a true man, in every sense of the word, was JAMES CHRISTIAN.

CHAPTER XII.

THE narrative which we have been pursuing has conducted us step by step to the close of the life of George Harris. Let us pause once more to take a cursory survey of the condition of affairs, as they presented themselves in the month of July, 1862, before we bring this sketch to a conclusion. The shattered and demoralized army of the Potomac, under command of McClellan, was now hugging the left bank of James river, and enjoying a temporary respite from active service under the protection of the monitors and other naval craft and gun-boats that held the river, and, from mortar and cannon, threw an arch of shot, shell, and other projectiles over the cudgelled and cowering Yankees that crouched and cringed behind their breastworks, and other defences along the river shore. The army of Northern Virginia, under command of General Lee, was still in camp around Richmond. General Jackson, ever restless and ever vigilant, was away with his hardy veterans watching the movements of General Pope, ready to come down like an avalanche upon his flank and rear, and send him back, as others had been sent before him, to tell the story of his defeat to his masters at Washington. Vicksburg was still holding out under the continuous bombardment from the Yankee gun-boats. "Jack Morgan" was spreading terror and consternation among the "Union men" in Kentucky. The Yankee Congress was trying to find out who was to blame for McClellan's failure to make good his "On to Richmond." The hospitals in and around Richmond, were crowded with the sick and wounded. Hundreds of the wounded Yankees were left in the hands of the Confederates. These occupied hospitals apart, specially assigned to them. From all parts of the South, fathers, and mothers, and wives were crowding to Richmond to nurse their wounded sons, and husbands, or to look for their graves on the battle-fields.

Old men were seen in eager search for their boys, who had actually walked hundreds of miles from their homes in distant parts of the country. Mothers and sisters were seen threading their way through the hospitals, or passing from hospital to hospital, in search of a wounded son or brother, as the case might be; and, failing to find the person looked for, these mothers, and sisters, and wives, were known to traverse the fields and woods, where the battles around the city were fought, with the vague hope of discovering some trace that might reveal the probable destiny of the object so earnestly and perseveringly sought. Every day witnessed some touching and beautiful exhibition of maternal love, or conjugal affection, or filial devotion. Were one scene of a hundred that were constantly transpiring committed to the canvas by the hands of competent and skilful artists, the most interesting gallery of memorial and historic paintings the world ever saw might be preserved for the wonder and admiration of the generations to come after us in the onward roll of time.

Colonel Harris had returned from his visit of search and inquiry, bearing the sad tidings to his family of the certain death of George. Suitable preparations were made for the transfer of his remains from Frazier's farm, to the family burying-ground in Albemarle. It was near the last of the month of July, when Colonel Harris, attended by a faithful servant, and his own little son, set out on this melancholy errand. On reaching the camp of the 19th Regiment, below Richmond, every facility was afforded the bereaved father that the kindness and courtesy of the officers and men could suggest or contrive, to aid him in his work. Quarter-Master Jones, a gentleman well known about Charlottesville, and the University of Virginia, ordered a neat coffin and box, and detailed a wagon and some soldiers, all of which was placed at the disposal of Colonel Harris for the disinterment and removal of the body of his son. A further detail of soldiers was made by the proper officer to attend the remains to Albemarle, with instructions that the brave and gallant soldier should be buried with military honors.

A touching incident occurred in connection with the removal of young Harris' remains. The camp of the 19th Regiment was about four miles below Richmond, and directly on the road leading to Frazier's farm; so that, after the disinterment of George's body, it had to be carried by the camp, *en route* for Richmond. As the wagon, with the escort, bearing the remains, approached the camp, the members of the company to which George belonged went out to meet the train, and, in silence, and in tears, with heads uncovered, they followed the wagon by the camp, and for some distance along the road beyond. Among the soldiers who paid this tribute to George Harris' remains, was a young man by the name of Martin, from Albemarle county. On his bare feet he walked a considerable distance from the camp in the direction of Frazier's farm to meet the lifeless body of his friend, and then followed the ambulance further than any one else in the direction of Richmond. This was an affecting tribute to the memory of a fellow-soldier, and was as grateful to the feelings of the father as it was creditable to the sentiments of the parties who paid this testimonial of affection to a fallen comrade in arms.

It was just one year from the day on which Bushrod Harris died at Centreville, to the day on which George Harris fell at Frazier's farm; the one dying on the 30th June 1861; the other being killed in battle on the 30th June 1862.

Suitable funeral solemnities were conducted on the occasion of the final reinterment of George Harris' remains in the old family burying-ground at Mountain Grove in Albemarle. A striking and impressive discourse was delivered on the occasion by the Rev. Joel Fortune, followed by a line of appropriate remarks by the Rev. Charles Wingfield. The latter spoke especially of the Christian character of the deceased, in which he narrated a conversation which he held with him just before he last left his home for the army, in which he gave unquestionable proof of an experimental knowledge of pardon and acceptance in the sight of God, and evinced all the scriptural marks of a due preparation to meet his final Judge in the event of his death.

The remarks of the reverend clergy present, and participating in the funeral services, were followed by an eloquent and beautiful tribute to his moral excellence as a Christian, and his heroic, and chivalrous daring and bravery as a soldier, by Captain Joseph Hopkins, who was the original captain of the company to which George Harris belonged, and who, as we have before seen, was present at the burial of Bushrod Harris, and delivered an appropriate eulogy on the occasion.

At the close of these solemnities the coffin containing all that was mortal of George N. Harris was lowered in the grave, side by side with his brother Bushrod. Their coffins were placed contiguous to each other; and, on refilling the grave, one mound marked the spot where the twin brothers sleep, in the silent house appointed for all the living. "They were lovely and pleasant in their lives, and in death they were not divided." They were pious and devout Christians at the time death summoned them away. They sleep in Jesus, and are destined to have a part in the first resurrection—the resurrection of the just.

A monumental marble slab stands above the slumbering dust of these young Christian soldiers, bearing the following inscription:

In memory of

BUSHROD W. AND GEORGE N. HARRIS,

Twin sons of

COL. G. W. AND M. M. HARRIS.

Born Jan. 11th, 1842.

B. W. HARRIS.
Died June 30th, 1861, at Centreville, a member of the 19th Va. Regmt. A soldier, and a Christian.
The last verse read by him was:
"But, we are not of those who draw back unto perdition, but of them that believe to the saving of the soul."

G. N. HARRIS
Died June 30th, 1862, on the battle-field of Fair Oaks. A member of the 19th Va. Regmt.
On Friday he led a victorious band—charged on the enemy, and captured Two Hundred and fifty.
"His work finished, he rests in the hope of a glorious Resurrection."

CHAPTER XIII.

We have followed the subjects of this Memorial Sketch through their brief career, from the cradle to the grave. How short the race! How contracted the span! "What is life? It is even a vapor that appeareth for a little time, and then vanisheth away." The cry of the ancient prophet still comes wailing along the lapse of the ages, as they glide away: "All flesh is grass, and all the glory of man as the flower of the grass: the grass withereth, and the flower thereof falleth away."

In monumental imagery and representation we sometimes find the marble shaft rudely broken, or the expanding flower snapped from its stem, designed to symbolize the early death of the young man of promise, suddenly cut down in the spring-time of life. The image is striking and impressive. The mute marble speaks to the heart. As we stand by the graves of the young men whose brief history has engaged our attention in these unpretending pages, we are ready to exclaim: "What hopes lie buried here!" Emerging from their youth and boyhood we find them on the edge of early manhood, just at the time the war for Southern independence was inaugurated by the secession of the Cotton States. They stand before us

with the dew of their youth upon them. The
one is the fac-simile of the other in form, and
feature. Manly in stature, ruddy in complexion, and vigorous in health, we see them
enter the Confederate service, full of life, animation, and hope. One of them had scarcely buckled on his armor, ere the arrow of the
fatal archer pierced "the joints of the harness," and he fell into the grave. The other
survived him just one year, when, suddenly,
while flushed with excitement and exhilarating hope, he was struck by the fatal ball, and,
in a moment—in the twinkling of an eye, he
was summoned to his final account, and to
his reward in another state of being. Happily, these youths were ready for the summons. They had been reared by pious parents. Their young feet had been trained in
the paths of early piety. They had been
taught to "remember their Creator in the days
of their youth." In the Sabbath-school they
had been instructed in the principles and precepts of our holy Christianity; and, on coming to more mature years, they adhered firmly to the principles of their early education.
Nor did they throw off the restraints of a
wholesome and scriptural morality on entering the army. With firmness and decision
of character they steadfastly resisted the
temptations of camp life, and maintained

their integrity even more conspicuously in the field than in the ordinary walks of life. They never fell into the vices so common in camp. The Sabbath was sacredly observed by them, as far as this was possible to privates in the ranks. Religious services, whenever accessible, were regularly attended by them. Private prayer was kept up, as a habit of life, as far as this was practicable in military service. They did not only reverence the name of God, but were chaste and pure in their conversation, and, at the same time abstained, habitually, from all those petty vices which are so common in camp; and in justification, or extenuation of which, the soldier never fails to find an apology, if not a full vindication, in the circumstances by which he is surrounded. And then, they were as brave as they were religious and correct in their morals. The character of the *soldier* is as fair and irreproachable in their history, as is the Christian character which they sustained. They were not less heroic and brave as soldiers, than they were firm and consistent as Christians. Hence, they were prepared for the Master's call, and as ready to do *his* bidding, as they were to wake at reveille, answer at roll-call, or charge the enemy at the word of command. In the old stone-church at Centreville, deep in the night, when the camp-fires were burning low, and silence and sleep were reigning in the camp, death laid his cold, skeleton hand on the heart of one of these youthful soldiers. Without alarm, or hesitation he yielded up his spirit into the hands of the God who gave it. He was not one of those who, having believed, "draw back to perdition; but, who believe to the saving of their souls." The other, "having fought a good fight and finished his course," fell at the opening of the terrific fight on Frazier's Farm, and instantly "laid hold on eternal life."

The climacteric point—the crowning incident in the soldier-life of George Harris, was the part he took in the storming of the enemy's stronghold at Gaines' Mill. We have attempted to set forth this valorous and unsurpassed deed of heroism without any exaggeration. Indeed, it might be put stronger than we have stated it. At the word of command given to the 19th Regiment to charge what seemed to be almost an impregnable position of the enemy—the position which formed the key to the line of defences along the crest of the hills, and which, once taken by the Confederates must decide the fortunes of McClellan's army—at the word of command to charge this point, after so many repulses, and after such terrible slaughter of our men,

George Harris bounded forward with such impetuosity as to clear the front of the line, and strode forward with such rapidity as to become separated from his company and his Regiment. Then it was he discovered the Texas and South Carolina Regiments before alluded to, closing in behind him, and by a mere accident, it would seem, he found himself leading these heroic men. The officers were cut down, and hundreds of the men reeled and fell under the murderous fire that was poured into the advancing column. George Harris still pressed forward, shouting to the brave men that kept their feet to "Come on;" and on they rushed, clambering up the rugged steeps. Presently young Harris was seen upon the highest point, with hat in hand, still shouting; "Come on, boys, —the day is ours." The battery that had been dealing death into the Confederate lines was silenced and captured, and George Harris was the first man to turn the guns upon the broken lines of the retreating foe. This was the *turning point* in the Seven Days' fighting around Richmond. The loss of that position necessitated retreat or surrender on the part of McClellan. Another *private soldier*, equally brave and daring as George Harris, *might* have been thrown in his position, and thus, by mere accident, as we say, been the leader in this last, successful charge; but, it so happened that *George Harris* was the man to whom this distinguished honor fell. Such deeds as he performed are above all praise; and, if dauntless courage, bold and dashing heroism, and brilliant achievements which turn the fortunes of the day in great decisive battles embalm the name of the *officer* who strikes the master-stroke, why should not the name of the private in the ranks, who displays similar traits, and performs equally noble and decisive deeds occupy as conspicuous a place in the scroll of fame? We will call GEORGE N. HARRIS *the hero of Gaines' Mill.*

As a further testimonial to the gallantry of young Harris, and as an additional confirmation of what has been said in the foregoing pages; we subjoin, in this connection, the following letter, addressed to Col. Harris:

Seven Islands, Va, Feby. 29, 1868.

Col. GEORGE HARRIS :

Having understood that you are preparing a history of the lives of your brave and noble sons, George, and Bushrod Harris, I deem it my duty to state that they were both as noble and brave men as honored our cause, at any time, during our struggle for independence. George Harris was *foremost in the gallant charge* made by Genl. Pickett's Brigade on the defences at Gaines' Mill, during the Seven Days' fighting around

Richmond. I was the officer in charge of the company of which he was a member, and, up to the time that I received my wound, he was discharging his duty *with more than usual gallantry*.

I am, Col., yours, most respectfully,
Dick Harlan.

Since the close of the war, a member of the First Texas Regiment, by the name of Skinner, who was reared in Virginia, but moved to Texas before the war, and thus became a member of the First Texas, by some mere accident was thrown at Col. Harris' residence in Albemarle. In conversation, he incidentally mentioned the fact that he was a member of the First Texas Regiment in the late war. He was asked if he was in the battle at Gaines' Mill. He replied that he was, and that he was in the desperate charge that carried the stronghold of the Yankees on the crest of the hills, which formed the crowning achievement of that hard-fought battle. He furthermore stated, in the course of the conversation, that *a young man*, not of their Regiment, led that charge. He did not know who the young man was—had a hundred times asked for information, but had never learned who he was, or from whence he came. His attention was directed to a large photograph likeness of George Harris, which was hanging in the room, and he instantly recognized it as the likeness of the person who led that bold, bloody and desperate, but successful charge at Gaines' Mill, on the 27th June, 1862.

While, on the one hand, we have endeavored to avoid fulsome and unmerited eulogy in speaking of the principal subject of the foregoing sketch, we have, on the other, honestly tried to do him full justice in all those instances where his valor, or his personal virtues seemed, for the time, to discriminate him from others, who, ordinarily were, in no way, inferior to him.

The following tribute to George N. Harris, supposed to have been written by his sister, and published in some of the papers, directly after his death, is herewith appended, as a sort of summary statement of the leading points in his life :

GEORGE N. HARRIS, son of Col. Geo. W. and Martha M. Harris, of Albemarle Co., Va., was born January 11th, 1842, and fell on the battle-field on Monday, June 30th, 1862. Thus hath another soldier fallen! At the first sound of the trump of war, he (with his twin-brother,) quitted the home of his childhood. They tore themselves away from the fond love of father, mother, and sisters, freely giving up all the promise of life for the defence of their country. While at Centreville, they were both attacked with measles. Bushrod W. Harris fell a victim to that disease ; and although George was very sick, still he soothed the dying pillow of his brother, and at his request read to him portions of Scriptures. On June 30th, 1861, his spirit quietly passed away, while in his brother's arms. Thus were brought home to their friends, who almost idolized them, two as noble and brave young soldiers as ever went in defence of their country, one a corpse, and the other so ill that for weeks he was laid on a bed of suffering, his friends despairing of his recovery.

Urged by a patriotic sense of duty, he wished to return before his health would admit of it, and was only restrained from doing so by the persuasion of his friends and Captain. The day after the Battle at Williamsburg he was detailed as a wagon-guard. When he heard the din of war, he asked permission to go back, and take a part in the battle, and would not rest until he was exchanged. His Captain made a note of it in his diary.

At Seven Pines he was detailed to guard some prisoners in the rear of the army. General Pickett ordered them to fall back, and as soon as he reached a place of safety, he took two men and rushed down upon the enemy and took ten prisoners. On Friday, June 27th, his regiment made two brilliant and successful charges upon the enemy. They stormed a battery, and he was the first man to put his hands upon a cannon and turn it upon the foe. At another time the order to charge was given, and he, with one of his company, went forward (all his officers being wounded), with the ardent spirit of enthusiasm, and undaunted perseverance in prosecuting the vast undertaking in which he was engaged. His voice could be heard above the roar of cannon, and the sound of musketry, bravely cheering and calling loudly, "Come on, boys, come on!" And brave and gallant men rushed to the sound of his all-animating and soul-inspiring voice, charged upon them, and conquered, captured and brought in two hundred and fifty prisoners.—Although surrounded by danger and death, he was shielded from all harm. Like Moses of old, with all the beauties of the earthly Canaan in his view, in a moment he was ushered into the glories of his heavenly inheritance, and in like manner, at the appointed time, having enjoyed three days of glorious triumph, (just twelve months after his brother died,) elated with success, as he was entering the battle-field, a random shot pierced his heart, and he died without a groan, and mingled in the armies of the skies. His father reached the battle-field on Wednesday after his death.—His grave could not be found. No one can conceive of the anguish of friends, thus to be kept in suspense for weeks. No one knew where George was. Nothing that affection could suggest was left undone to find him out. His father fortunately met with a fellow-soldier who saw him fall, and directed him to his grave. His precious body was not suffered to remain on the battle-field, but was brought home to repose in the same grave with his loving and much-loved brother. Capt. Hopkins (their former captain) superintended his burial, as he had done his brother's with military honors, and with feelings uncontrollable, made some touching and beautiful remarks, that drew tears from every eye. Their affections were warm and generous, which attached them firmly to their family and friends. Their high sense of honor restrained them from every course of conduct not consistent with the character of true followers of Christ. Their tender regard for the feelings of others endeared them to all : and if the universal testimony of their companions in arms is of any avail, the corruptions of camp-life served but to refine and elevate their souls. They were members of the 19th Regiment Va. Volunteers. Lovely and pleasant in their lives, and in death they were not divided.

They rest in peace. No more will the sound of the drum call them to the tented field. No more will the clarion notes of the bugle arouse their patriotic souls and urge them on to deeds of noble daring. No more will the roar of cannon fall on their ears, now cold in death.

Sleep on, my brothers, till the trump of God shall arouse your slumbering dust, surrounded by a halo of heavenly glory, and ascend to the armies of the skies. Farewell, my dear brothers, till the resurrection morn.

JULIETTA.

CHAPTER XV.

WHO will ever be able to approach even to an approximate estimate of the havoc created by the ravages of the late war? Take a single neighborhood, and a single company. Our narrative leads us to Company D of the 19th Regiment Virginia Volunteers. How few of this company that started from Howardsville in the month of May, 1861, saw the close of the war! Bushrod Harris fell a victim to disease before the leaves on the trees of the first summer of the war had reached full size. Samuel Thurmond died directly after the first battle at Manassas. He was as true a man, and as brave a soldier as ever pulled a trigger, or shared a scanty ration with a comrade in arms. W. W. Walton, and Wm. H. Thomas were killed at the battle of Williamsburg, on the 5th of May, 1862. They were noble and patriotic young men, and died only as heroes die, at the post of duty, in the hottest of the fight. William D. Harris was killed on the 1st of

June, at the battle of Seven Pines. He was among the bravest that fell in that murderous fight. Wm. A. Moss, and John Barston were killed on the 27th June, in the desperate charges made by Pickett's Brigade at Gaines' Mill. Braver men never fought or fell, than fell that day. And oh! how rapidly they fell. Col. Robert E. Withers, who was in command of the 18th Virginia Regiment, and who received not less than three wounds in the brief space of a few moments, says that, in one of these charges made by Pickett's Brigade he lost *two hundred and ten men,* in his regiment, in ten minutes' time! How terrific! How appalling! A. R. Seay, and George N. Harris were killed on the 30th of June at Frazier's farm. Robert C. Fortune was wounded at Seven Pines, and died in camp below Richmond. One of his brothers was killed at Gettysburg, and still another died of disease while in military service. These were all young men of great promise—of high moral worth as citizens, and of dauntless courage as soldiers. And these are but a few of the many that fell in that one company. Then how many were wounded! How many lost limbs! How many will go to their graves on crutches! If such is the record of a single company, what pen can describe the sum-total of sufferings, and death, and maiming which were occasioned by the horrid havoc of the war?

Colonel Harris, in speaking on the subject which is just now engaging our attention, says: "I have thought it might not be out of place to speak of the privations and sufferings of the soldiers, and soldiers' families, within the sound of a horn around my residence. Peter P. Turner, after undergoing the hardships peculiar to the 'Valley service,' was captured and imprisoned for many months, during which time incurable damage was inflicted on his constitution. James Baler and William Powell also suffered extremely in Yankee prisons. My neighbor, Jacob Powell, lost two gallant sons in battle in the course of three days. Andrew J. Dawson was wounded a third time, then captured, and had a leg amputated in prison. My widowed sister, Mrs. R. Harris, had three sons in the service. One was wounded in the Williamsburg fight, subsequently attacked with measles, and died on his way home: Another was captured, near Petersburg, and suffered much in prison. James Christian and Ben Anderson were killed at Boonsboro. Captain George Killian was detained in prison fourteen months. Rev. Joel Fortune lost three of his sons in the army—one died of disease, and the others fell in battle. John Elsom, after rendering valuable and heroic service was instantly shot dead, while engaged in a fight. Mrs. Morris had four sons in the army. Two died in the service, and a third had his arm shot off close to his body. Andrew and James Brown (brothers) were severely wounded, but recovered. My neighbor, Colonel William M. Peyton, suffered immensely from depredations commited on his effects in his removal from New York to his native State. James Hamner, after remaining in prison for thirteen months was discharged, and anxious friends were awaiting his return home. Direct intelligence, as it appeared to be, was received by his wife and family to the effect that, while on his return by a steamer he had died at sea, and his body had been consigned to a watery grave. Happily the intelligence turned out to be false, and in the course of the next ten days the disconsolate wife, and unhappy children, had the inexpressible pleasure of greeting the husband and father on his unexpected return to his home.

"From my door-step I can almost cast my eye over the entire area of country in which all that I have just described transpired during the war. And if the country, generally, suffered as did the section immediately around me, what mind can conceive of the aggregate of calamity, suffering, desolation, widowhood, orphanage, sorrow and death occasioned by the war?"

The foregoing narrative of the casualties and disasters occurring in a single neighborhood as detailed by Colonel Harris, may be regarded as a sort of average sample of what occurred in the Southern states generally. In some neighborhoods it was even worse—in others not so bad, but every where sufficiently appalling to make the heart grow sick in the survey of the black and bloody war-path that still may be traced, in every direction, over these battle-scarred, and desolated lands. The genius of Southern chivalry, and of Southern independence, is aptly symbolized by the voice heard in Rama: "Lamentation, and weeping, and great mourning, Rachel weeping for her children, and would not be comforted, *because they are not.*"

We have had occasion in the foregoing pages to make some allusions to the "Home Guards," commanded by Captain Samuel Garland, afterwards the gallant Colonel of the Eleventh Virginia Regiment, who fell at the battle of Boonsboro, and to the "Rifle Grays," commanded by Captain Maurice Langhorne, and to other companies that left Lynchburg for Richmond in the month of May, 1861. The reader will indulge us in a brief reference to another company that performed conspicuous service, and whose roll presents a bloody record.

At the time of the departure of the above mentioned companies from Lynchburg, a *cavalry* company, known as the " Wise Troop," was in camp in a beautiful grove of oaks skirting the western suburbs of the city. This company had been organized under the command of Captain R. C. W. Radford, and was made up principally of young men from Lynchburg, and the surrounding counties. It numbered about eighty men at the time it was mustered into the Confederate service. Captain Radford was succeeded in command of the company by Captain J. S. Longhorne, before the company broke up camp and started to the field.

On the morning of the 3d of June, the *Wise Troop* came into the city, paraded through its principal streets, and halted near the Orange and Alexandria Railroad depot for an hour or two before taking up the line of march in the direction of Manassas, at which point the Confederate army was massing and organizing for the impending conflict. The *Wise Troop* was a splendid and admirably equipped company. Every man was handsomely accoutred, and well mounted. The elegant and high-blooded horses were finely caparisoned. In *physique*, as in *morale*, the men this company were unsurpassed. They were indeed the pride and the flower of Lynchburg and the surrounding country. Their new uniforms and glistening arms, furbished to the last degree of polish, shone resplendently in the clear light of that bright and beautiful June morning. The occasion was full of touching interest. Young wives, and mothers, and sisters were deeply interested spectators, as the clattering of sabres, and the rattling of carbines, and the gingling of spurs announced the mounting of the men for their final departure from the city. The partings were in silence and in tears. There was an attempt at a sort of gayety and cheerfulness on the part of the soldiery; but, unbidden tears dimmed the eyes of the bravest of them as the last farewells were exchanged with friends who were to be left behind. Well do we remember now the faces that met our glance as the eye wandered along the line; faces that were familiar, beaming with intelligence, and linked with many fond recollections in the social relations of life. But where are those faces now? Those manly forms, where? Out of the eighty who formed the original company, and who *remained in connection with the company, sharing its fortunes during the war*, it is said but six or seven, at most, came out of the contest alive. A number were transferred to other companies, and to other departments of military service, some of whom still live, but only six of those who remained in the company escaped death— being overtaken either in the conflict with the foe, or dying of diseases contracted in the camp.

Among the many that fell, we recall a *James Chalmers*, who was a brave soldier, and a sincere Christian. There was a simplicity and beauty about his character, a gentleness and fascination about his manners, and a granite firmness about his principles, that commanded the respect, and won the confidence of all that knew him. He was shot on picket-duty, how, or by whom, is enveloped in mystery. He was as pure and true a man as ever lived. "None knew him but to love him." His comrades in arms wept over his lifeless remains, as if a brother had fallen. His funeral solemnities, in Lynchburg, were touching and impressive.

William Stratton, too, was a noble specimen of a man. Tall in stature, handsome in person, agreeable in his deportment, and generous in his nature, his name was never mentioned but in praise. He fell only as the brave and daring fall. His memory is precious to those who knew him well.

Caleb Shearer, another member of this company, was as good a man as ever graced humanity. He was quiet, gentle, and unobtrusive, but as heroic in battle as any man that ever drew a blade. His virtues bound all hearts to him while living; and "being dead he yet speaketh." His example survives him, and will long continue to exert a silent but powerful influence in the circles where he was known and esteemed.

Richard Tyree, and William Cross, were also honored and highly esteemed members of this company, both of whom fell at the post of duty. A sad vacancy was occasioned in the home-circle when the first-mentioned of these two young men was cut down; and a happy household was rendered inconsolable when the tidings came that the last-mentioned was among the dead. The above named gentlemen, members of the Wise Troop, were from Lynchburg or its immediate vicinity. Others there may have been—most probably were, in this company not now recalled, equally brave and heroic with those whose names we have recorded, whose death has left an appalling gloom on other hearths and homes, in and around Lynchburg. But time would fail us to enumerate all who were connected with the Wise Troop, who fell in the war; and the vocabulary in which we utter eulogy would be exhausted in the attempt to pay the justly-merited tribute to their private worth as citizens, and to their courage, patriotism, and bravery as soldiers.

There is one, however, that we should be inexcusable in passing by without notice, since we have mentioned the names of others of the original members of this company that were cut down in active service. We allude to *Edward W. Horner*, who was lieutenant of the company at the time he received his death wound, in a gallant charge upon the enemy. Colonel Munford, who was in command of the 2d Regiment Virginia Cavalry, of which Lt. Horner was a member, in writing to the father of the young man, announcing his death, uses the following language: " Your son, by his gallant bearing, and genial manners, had won the respect of his entire command, and, it will at least be a comfort to you to be assured that he fell at the *very head* of his command, with his arms uplifted, cheering on his men, and striking for his country." To this high testimonial of Col. Munford, Captain Charles M. Blackford, who had, until shortly before the death of Lieut. Horner, been, for some time, in command of the company to which Horner belonged, adds the following beautiful and touching tribute to him as a man, and as a soldier: "I think I may say

I knew him well. From the beginning to the end of this intimacy I never had, on one single occasion, to wish that his condnct as a soldier, as an officer, as a gentleman, or as a friend, had been, in any respect, different from what it was. Higher praise than this I cannot give to any man. It is needless for me to tell you, as his father, how kind, how gentle, how womanly he was; and, his gallant death-charge proved that yet, with all, a lion's heart made him the chivalrous soldier."

The following young gentlemen are the six survivors in this ill-fated company—namely: A. Sidney Watson, son of Dr. Daniel Watson, of Albemarle, Virginia, J. L. Massie, Daniel Luck, R. D. Isbell, R. W. Lacy, and T. W. Allen. These, *all*, sustained the very highest reputation as soldiers during the whole war. They were in many skirmishes, and had a part in nearly all the great cavalry fights of the protracted conflict, and yet they came out without loss of limb, and still live to grace the private walks of life with their social virtues, as they were an ornament to the ranks as brave and intrepid soldiers. The few that survive the many, must "feel a touch of sorrow" as they recall the forms and faces that have gone down to the dust since that cloudless morning in June, 1861, when the company answered roll-call just on the eve of their departure from Lynchburg. As we have said, some were transferred to other departments of military service, some were promoted—some were discharged, but, oh! how many were slain, or fell of disease contracted in the army! How few whose names formed the original roll of the company stood on that roll at the end of the war, without an erasure, or explanatory entry opposite the name!

But, we pause. The memorial sketch which has engaged our attention in these pages, might have been recorded in briefer space, but, we have been led to expand the incidents connected with the lives of the young men whose short history it has been our special object to narrate, into a volume, by interweaving with them the concurring, coincident, and concomitant events of the times in which they lived. The volume itself, is designed by the *father* of the " twin-brothers" to be *monumental;* and while the *names* of his sons are inscribed prominently, and conspicuously upon the monumental page, he has, nevertheless, endeavored, as far as anything like *unity* in the work would allow, to introduce the names at least of some of the associates and comrades of his sons upon these pages, with the design of perpetuating the memory and deeds of a portion of the Confederate soldiery, who, in all probability, but for this memorial offering would pass into silence and forgetfulness, without leaving a solitary remembered trace that they ever had a being.

After all, is not a *book* as fitting a monument as the marble or granite shaft? The material of which the book is made is less durable than the marble. The characters chiselled in on the face of the pedestal that supports the column, or inscribed on the surface of the slab that covers the grave, may be less easily effaced than the printer's ink that marks the name on the frail and perishable page of a little book. But still the *book*, frail as is its material, will perpetuate the names and noble deeds of men, when the abrasions of time shall have blotted the epitaph, and ground to impalpable powder the marble on which it was inscribed. Books live in libraries, and in the memories of men, and are transmitted from generation to generation. Books are reproduced by the magic power of the press. Books gain admittance to the hearths and homes of the people of all lands, and meet the eyes of the Million. Marble monuments are seen but by the few whom chance may throw into the cemetery, or private burying-ground where they stand with their brief records. The book is every way as impressive and appropriate as a monument, as the elaborate marble pile.

We take occasion, therefore, in closing up this tribute to *Bushrod Washington* and *George Nelson Harris*, to express our high sense of admiration of the affection and the sentiments that prompted a devoted and patriotic father to perpetuate the names and deeds of his soldier-sons in a *book*, however small and unpretending, rather than in the sculptured urn, and the monumental bust. The twin-brothers were *par nobile fratrum*. They deserve a higher eulogy than is contained in these pages; but what pen can trace the tribute due to the CONFEDERATE SOLDIER?

www.ingramcontent.com/pod-product-compliance
Lightning Source LLC
Chambersburg PA
CBHW030356170426
43202CB00010B/1389